Entrepreneurship in Action

Entrepreneurship in Action

The Power of Student-Run Ventures

Edited by

Eric W. Liguori

Rohrer Endowed Chair of Entrepreneurship and Executive Director, Center for Innovation and Entrepreneurship, Rohrer College of Business, Rowan University, USA

Mark Tonelli

Assistant Professor of Music and coordinator of guitar studies, College of Fine Arts, Millikin University, USA

Edward Elgar
PUBLISHING

Cheltenham, UK • Northampton, MA, USA

Published by
Edward Elgar Publishing Limited
The Lypiatts
15 Lansdown Road
Cheltenham
Glos GL50 2JA
UK

Edward Elgar Publishing, Inc.
William Pratt House
9 Dewey Court
Northampton
Massachusetts 01060
USA

Paperback edition 2022

A catalogue record for this book
is available from the British Library

Library of Congress Control Number: 2020950923

This book is available electronically in the **Elgar**online
Business subject collection
http://dx.doi.org/10.4337/9781839102943

ISBN 978 1 83910 293 6 (cased)
ISBN 978 1 83910 294 3 (eBook)
ISBN 978 1 0353 0027 3 (paperback)

Printed and bound by CPI Group (UK) Ltd, Croydon, CR0 4YY

Contents

Notes on contributors

Dave Burdick is an Associate Professor in the School of Music at Millikin University (USA).

Kate Flemming is a Change Management Strategist with Sanford Health in Sioux Falls, SD (USA).

Stephen Frech is a Professor in the English Department at Millikin University (USA).

Eric W. Liguori is the Rohrer Endowed Chair of Entrepreneurship and Executive Director of the Center for Innovation and Entrepreneurship at Rowan University. He served as President of the United States Association for Small Business and Entrepreneurship in 2019 (USA).

RJ Podeschi is an Associate Professor of Information Systems in the Tabor School of Business at Millikin University (USA).

Julienne Shields is the Chief Executive Officer of the United States Association for Small Business and Entrepreneurship. Prior to this role she was the Director of the Center for Entrepreneurship at Millikin University (USA).

Sara Theis is an Associate Professor of Arts Administration and Stage Management in the School of Theatre and Dance at Millikin University (USA).

Mark Tonelli is an Assistant Professor of Music in the School of Music at Millikin University (USA).

Lee Zane is an Associate Professor of Entrepreneurship in the Rohrer College of Business at Rowan University (USA).

James Zebrowski is the Executive Director of the Collegiate Entrepreneurs' Organization (CEO) (USA).

Editorial review board

Foreword

Right around the time Steve Jobs was attending Reed College in the early 1970s, and just as he dropped-out to join his local Homebrew Computer Club, discussions regarding the necessity of entrepreneurship programming on university and college campuses began. At this time, if a professor were to express the desire to implement entrepreneurship programming, the proposal was immediately met with resistance. The verses made debate of whether entrepreneurship could be taught and/or nurtured, or if it was a natural trait, and there were strong proponents backing both sides. To further the challenge, there was no generally accepted conceptualization of what entrepreneurial characteristics were, let alone a way to measure or demonstrate they had been learned, which led to a lot of discussion from what was then a small group of academics.

As these discussions progressed, partners such as the Coleman, Hughes, and Kauffman Foundations joined the conversation. These three organizations helped usher in a different approach to getting entrepreneurship programming established on campuses across the nation. They recognized that advocating for the importance of entrepreneurship programming to university leadership wasn't likely to gain meaningful traction nor push the needle. Faced with this reality, they turned the model on its head, and instead of working top-down they began to work bottom-up by offering programming to the students. This led to the creation of the Collegiate Entrepreneurs' Organization (CEO), which sought to infuse campuses with co-curricular entrepreneurial experiences by way of new venture creation. The founders theorized that by creating groups of students with a shared interest in business development, senior administration would have no choice but to act and support this discipline. Over time, the approach proved effective. Today, entrepreneurship is a recognized and established discipline with a robust set of pedagogical tools emphasizing exploratory and experiential approaches. Moreover, entrepreneurship education and programming has woven itself into the fabric of many universities and countless disciplines, with students from virtually every major and on most every campus now having opportunities to develop both mindsets and skillsets for entrepreneurship. Looking back, it is almost ironic that right around the time Steve Jobs dropped-out of college, an organization, one he likely would have been quite interested in, was starting to really blossom.

Across the variety of campuses in the CEO network, many chapters have created revenue generating models via student-run ventures. Examples of this include regional conferences, coffee shops, laundering, cleaning, event production, and start-up consultant services. These businesses provide real, actionable experience to the students in the program. When CEO evaluates a student venture, we're looking for more than just how they execute on the business model, we're looking into the students themselves. When you pair a co-curricular experience such as running a business, with actionable curriculum and the guidance of a professor, the marriage leads to a stronger continuousness of the venture and an increased likelihood of the student's future success.

If your campus is already running a student venture, you undoubtedly understand the impact it has left among thousands of students. The real-world learnings are undeniable. For a professor, observing a student create opportunities for their colleagues is arguably one of the most rewarding experiences you can have. Understanding that you've unlocked their ability to create something from nothing, sustaining operations, and/or growing the business is a sign of a true learning proficiency. Millikin University, with the support of the Coleman Foundation, has long embraced the impact of student run ventures on their campus and its outcomes are evident.

As you dive deeper into this book you will explore first-hand accounts of student-run ventures, complete with both faculty and student reflection. Not every case summary claims to be wildly successful, nor are all the cases presented still in operation (though most are). We inherently learn from failure, and we know sometimes certain business models run their course. This book presents a picture of reality more than it does utopia. It offers candid perspectives on best practices, new methodologies, and how the student-run venture experience can help to expand the mind of student entrepreneurs. As someone who works daily to help student clubs and organizations succeed, I know first-hand that while students may see many successes, they learn the most from failures, and this is what propels them to continually improve.

If, like me, you teach entrepreneurship or work with aspiring student entrepreneurs, you already know the likelihood of students immediately launching a viable venture post-graduation is limited. Many of the ventures launched while enrolled will not make it. However, students continue to learn as they enter their desired industry. Along their journey they may create a solution for a void in their market. This is why we must be relentless in the charge of supporting co-curricular learning models that encourage action. Learning today – by way of participating in a student-run venture, supported by a faculty member, and university infrastructure (this is key) – teaches the interworkings of new venture creation to students in a way much more powerful than most any classroom lecture or textbook can. In this sense, like most entrepreneurs, we have to focus on the long term, not pat ourselves on the back for short term successes.

For nearly 36 years CEO has witnessed the irrepressible desire to become entrepreneurs evident in countless students on campuses around the globe. These aspiring entrepreneurs are go-getters, visionaries, and very likely the next generation of business leaders. Anything we can do to support these select students, as well as inspire more of their peers to join them, should be a mission-critical goal of higher education. Looking to the future there is no shortage of problems to be solved, so, the sooner we can empower future generations of students to become value-creators and creative problem solvers the sooner we can begin to tackle these challenges. Value creation, problem solving, these are the essence of entrepreneurship. CEO has more than 16,000 members on over 250 campuses and it is students like these that prove the power of student-run ventures and entrepreneurial action each and every day.

James Zebrowski
Executive Director, Collegiate Entrepreneurs' Organization

Acknowledgements

This book would not have been possible if it were not for Sharon Alpi and Julienne Shields championing student-run ventures at Millikin University and Millikin University Leadership who have supported these ventures throughout their lifecycles. Countless students have expressed their thanks for the life-changing opportunities these student-run ventures have afforded them. In addition, the Editors thank Michael Luchies for his substantive contributions and insights which helped shape the totality of this volume and Katelyn Laudone for her input on the design of the cover.

Additionally, the Editors wish to thank the following individuals and organizations for their support, feedback, and inspiration: Alan Sturmer, Fiona Briden, Edward Elgar Publishing, Rowan University, Millikin University, Sue Lehrman, Morris Kalliny, Cheryl Bodnar, Lee Zane, Susana Santos, Michael Dominik, Jessica Vattima, Greg Payton, Doan Winkel, Josh Bendickson, James Zebrowski, the Collegiate Entrepreneurs' Organization, Jeff Vanevenhoven, Wendy Plant, Heidi Neck, the United States Association for Small Business and Entrepreneurship (USASBE), James Hart, Ayman El Tarabishy, the International Council for Small Business (ICSB), Rebecca Corbin, the National Association for Community College Entrepreneurship (NACCE), Michael Hennessy, the Coleman Foundation, and the Hughes Foundation.

PART I

Contemporary perspectives on student-run ventures

1. Entrepreneurship in action: the power of the student-run venture

Mark Tonelli

Investing in a decade's worth of education takes commitment. This commitment, in my experience at least, stems from inspiration. In the 1980s, as a teenager, I looked up to my high school choir teacher. He had a knack for connecting with students and shared about his efforts to complete his doctorate in piano performance while teaching. I wanted to follow in his footsteps, and this inspired me to pursue a doctorate. It's safe to say that I didn't know what I was in for.

Every doctoral student faces the same challenging question – "What should my dissertation be about?" It's a question I asked myself frequently, even before beginning my doctorate journey. I imagined choosing a topic tied to music performance or music education. But the world started to change, and my interests and what I saw as necessary shifted. As I began my doctoral work, I realized that people communicated, shopped, relaxed, ate, and essentially lived differently. Why? Because of technology.

Technology, particularly the internet, had changed everything. In turn, that change caused a shift in the way people work. The traditional model of graduating from college and working loyally for the same company for the next 30 years was beginning to vanish. In its place, fueled by technology, economic volatility, and globalization, the concept of being an entrepreneur began to emerge. College students needed to learn skills for their respective fields, know how to create their own work, identify opportunities in rapidly shifting markets, and discover how to be resilient, adaptable, and flexible. In other words, this edition of college students needed to reinvent themselves, like how the world of the 21st century reinvented itself.

This trend was just one of many I was trying to decode. I also came to realize that while I received the best musical training you could buy, I did not receive training on how to translate those hard-earned musical skills into a sustainable career. There were no courses on music entrepreneurship or a "do-it-yourself" music career. I had been guided towards my passion but not necessarily given instruction on how to forge a sustainable career path.

The "business" aspects of a music career were not on anyone's radar at this time. We were primarily concerned with being the best musicians – convinced somehow that our superior musical skills would "get us noticed" and lead to financial success. You know, it was that old chestnut of being in the right place at the right time, and believing that if you worked hard enough on your craft, you would succeed.

Once I completed graduate school in 2000 and began my professional career, I waited for the job offers to start pouring in. They came but only in spurts and not as steadily as I had imagined. It was not long before I realized that if I wanted to have a career as an artist, I would have to create that career myself. This began my on-the-job education of learning to create opportunities for myself.

I was not alone. I soon discovered that friends and colleagues in the industry were having similar struggles, and together we cried, "We were not prepared for this!" After ten years in the trenches, I began to see a need for reform in music education. Students needed to prepare for their new reality. They will have to create their own careers; they will have to become entrepreneurs as well as artists.

These observations culminated in a worthy topic for my dissertation. I would study how entrepreneurship was taught in college music programs, and to what level it impacted the potential of a musician. It wasn't a topic I had ever considered before coming to the revelation that some of the most talented musicians did not know how to create opportunities to showcase their talent. This meant that all the musical training in the world would not matter to them without instruction on how to turn that skill and passion into a sustainable career or business.

My research concluded that integrating entrepreneurship in college music programs is valuable and makes a positive difference in the careers of students. This is not an abstract concept. It applies directly to my own career. Even though I now teach full-time, I continue to be entrepreneurial. I create opportunities for my ensemble to perform, publish music instructional books, write a blog, present at conferences, post on social media, record new music, and constantly network. If I ever stopped doing these things, my career would stagnate, and I, as a music performance and entrepreneurship professor, would no longer be relevant. After all, professors and institutions must innovate along with the rest of the world to fulfill the needs of their students.

A few years ago, I arrived at Millikin University as an entrepreneurial musician. Millikin University, an institution that *breathes* entrepreneurship, was founded in 1901 as a small, private institution located south of Chicago in Decatur, Illinois. The school is small with enrollment of around 2,000 undergraduate and 90 graduate students. The university is known for its arts, nursing, and business programs, including entrepreneurship.

At the time, Millikin's entrepreneurial engine was primarily fueled by the Center for Entrepreneurship (CFE), led by Director Julie Shields and Coordinator Kate Flemming, who both have made significant contributions to the entrepreneurial success at Millikin and this book. I felt an instant connection to the CFE and agreed to serve on a planning committee for the national conference of the Society for Arts Entrepreneurship Education (SAEE). It was during the SAEE conference, hosted at Millikin, that I began to discover a new world – the student-run venture. I attended a panel organized by Sara Theis, who teaches Pipe Dreams Studio Theatre, a student-run venture in which students run a black box theatre. The panel was composed of current and former students who discussed the profound impact Pipe Dreams had or was having on their careers and development. After the conference, the planning committee reviewed surveys completed by attendees. The Pipe Dreams panel session and the student-run venture concept was mentioned over and over as a highlight for attendees. It was clear that something special was happening at Millikin with our student-run ventures.

WHAT IS A STUDENT-RUN VENTURE (SRV)?

A student-run venture allows students to earn college credit for learning how to run a business by running a business. They get hands-on experience by taking over the operations of a fully functioning business. As discussed in Chapter 13, I eventually created my own student-run venture, Arts Café, and have become part of the community of student-run ventures at Millikin.

Through my fellowship with the Coleman Foundation, which supports entrepreneurship education in academia, I have also had the opportunity to meet and work with Coleman Fellows on Millikin's campus, and learn about their student-run ventures. Creating a network of educators all focused on enhancing entrepreneurship education through student-run ventures has helped us guide stronger student-run ventures on our campus while allowing us to share our successes and failures to help others.

Millikin currently has 15 student-run ventures, nearly double the number of ventures as when I arrived in 2016. As I observe the work of my colleagues who teach other student-run ventures, I am impressed by the scope and relevance of what they are doing. Collectively, our students acquire critical skills and accelerate their learning in a way that is not possible without student-run ventures. Through experiential learning in a real business on campus, students get relevant and valuable experience in a low-risk environment while earning college credit.

As I considered the breadth and quality of my colleagues' work, the impact it was having on our students' development and success, and the interest that entrepreneurship educators had with our student-run ventures at the SAEE conference, it occurred to me that our work could be valuable to a wider audience. Why should this model and these approaches stay within the walls of Millikin University when millions of students around the world could benefit greatly from student-run ventures?

Entrepreneurship in Action: The Power of the Student-Run Venture should be utilized as a guide to draw from similar, yet vastly different approaches to teaching students how to develop entrepreneurship skills. Millikin's work has broad application across multiple academic disciplines, and we are excited to make this information available to impact your teaching, institution, and most importantly, your students.

Each case in this book discusses one of six different student-run ventures at Millikin University, with each being led by a different professor with their own unique approach. Emerging from their pedagogy are themes that exemplify the work they are doing.

Meet your other student-run venture guides:

Dave Burdick, Art Circus, a Performance Art Group

- Opportunity recognition
- Impact feasibility
- Vision

Kate Flemming, Blue Connection, an Art Gallery

- Creative entrepreneurial collisions
- "Drinking from a firehose" structure
- Customer–gallery–artist triangle
- Exploring new organizational tools

Sara Theis, Pipe Dreams Studio Theatre, a Black Box Theatre

- Listening
- Pivoting
- Intervention

RJ Podeschi, MU Performance Consulting, an IT Business

- How technology-based SRVs are different from traditional business model SRVs
- Strategies for sustainability in SRVs, knowledge transfer
- Balance between hands-on and hands-off as a faculty advisor/leader of a SRV

Mark Tonelli, Arts Café, a Live Performance Venue

- Selling an experience
- Consistently delivering a high-quality product
- Developing leadership abilities in students

Just as our students learn lessons from each of our student-run ventures that they can apply to future careers and businesses, you will find information, approaches, and new tools that you can apply to your unique instructional context, whether it is in the arts or business, secondary or post-secondary education. You will find both highly individualized approaches to teaching SRVs as well as recurrent themes that surface across chapters. The principles embodied in these themes can be transferred and employed by teachers across multiple disciplines with students in a variety of situations in macro and nuanced scenarios. Put simply, this book has a lot to offer you, regardless of your program's current makeup.

Are you new to SRVs? If you have never taught a student-run venture, then you will find a wealth of enlightenment for starting one using our 50+ years of combined experience teaching student-run ventures. As I learned in my time at Millikin, starting and teaching a student-run venture is not as challenging as you might think, and incredibly rewarding for you, the school community, and your students. We have packed this book full of everything you need to learn about SRVs, compare approaches, and gain new ideas that will help you take away what works for you. Whether you decide to launch an SRV at your institution or just dip your toes into the entrepreneurship instruction pool outside of post-secondary education – come on in, the water's fine, and there are lifeguards standing by to help!

Don't just take our word for it. You will also read about the experiences of Millikin graduates who were formerly enrolled in student-run ventures. They tell it in their own words, providing the big picture of how student-run ventures can have a positive impact on graduates' careers. Their experiences, combined with the knowledge of our instructors, make this book a valuable resource. I hope it will be a source of tools, strategies, and inspiration for you and your future as an entrepreneurship educator.

2. Student-run ventures and interdisciplinary entrepreneurship education

Eric W. Liguori and Lee Zane

We live in an exciting era for entrepreneurship education, one where entrepreneurship education has become ubiquitous in higher education and is nearing ubiquity in education more broadly. Countless K-12 programs have added entrepreneurship courses and modules to their curriculums. The National Association for Community College Entrepreneurship, the United States Association for Small Business and Entrepreneurship, and the International Council for Small Business, all three of which are leading academic membership organizations supporting entrepreneurship education, boast more members than they have at any other time in their histories. Moreover, it is estimated that more than 5,000 institutions offer entrepreneurship education programs around the globe (Liguori, Corbin, Lackeus, & Solomon, 2019), with steady growth happening each year and little to no attrition in sight.

This growth and ubiquity is attributable to multiple factors. First, given entrepreneurial activity is a major determinant of economic development and growth (Schumpeter, 1934; Stevenson & Sahlman, 1986; Birch, 1987; Baumol & Strom, 2007), academia has rightfully and logically built programs focusing on the topic. A complementary explanation for entrepreneurship's proliferation in education is academia's realization that entrepreneurship is an interdisciplinary topic at its core. Certainly, business schools grew entrepreneurship programs to the point of critical mass in higher education, something that was arguably accomplished in the 1990s and early 2000s. This growth makes sense – business is, largely, the result of entrepreneurship, and the elements of entrepreneurship happen daily in the business world.

Over the last decade, however, the growth has been broader, with more and more university leaders recognizing that students from all disciplines benefit from developing entrepreneurial mindsets and understanding the fundamentals of topics such as opportunity recognition and value creation. Similarly, more and more K-12 educators and policy makers have recognized the need and benefit of cultivating entrepreneurial mindset at a younger age.

Thus, the growth that has happened over the last 10 years or so is much more boundary-spanning and interdisciplinary than what we experienced in the two decades prior. In many cases, academia has used entrepreneurship as a mechanism to begin to break down traditional silos and build bridges between disciplines, and deployment of entrepreneurship education in the K-12 space has maintained an interdisciplinary nature.

The dynamic nature of this growth has led entrepreneurship education to be a space where people from a wide variety of backgrounds have been tasked with teaching a singular topic, typically with disparate expertise on the topic. This disparity, coupled with the relative youth of entrepreneurship as an academic discipline, has led to a lack of consistency in content and approach inside the modern entrepreneurship classroom. This inconsistency noted, most educators do emphasize some sort of experiential learning (e.g., Falk & Alberti, 2000; Greene, Katz, & Johannisson, 2004). Research into entrepreneurship education has begun to deliberately explore what happens in the classroom, assessing the effectiveness of different learning models and interventions. While the results have been varied, trends have emerged, and overall there is a reasonable level of consensus that entrepreneurship education should focus on real-world experience, be action-oriented, practice-based, and harness the learning power of reflection (cf. Kassean, Vanevenhoven, Liguori, & Winkel, 2015; Neck & Green, 2011; Neck, Green, & Brush, 2014; Vanevenhoven & Liguori, 2013). Morris and Liguori (2016) go so far as to suggest that as much as 60% of entrepreneurship classroom time should center around experiential learning and deliberate practice, but that a bold percentage challenges the convention of traditional models of education.

This is where student-run ventures enter. In this sense, student-run ventures are great mechanisms to teach entrepreneurship to students. They are the definition of action-oriented and practice-based, are very much connected to the real world, and create powerful experiences that enable meaningful reflection. A student-run venture can be defined many ways, but essentially, we're talking about student-led/managed/controlled ventures with (ideally) sustainable revenue models that perform services or provide products to real customers. Julienne Shields, Chief Executive Officer of the United States Association for Small Business and Entrepreneurship and former Director of the Center for Entrepreneurship at Millikin University, characterizes these ventures as laboratories of practice grounded in an academic discipline. The purpose of these ventures is simple: to engage students in authentic learning, which should lead to greater entrepreneurial abilities and propensity, and eventually to enhanced entrepreneurial performance, which benefits individuals and societies.

More critically, student-run ventures are safe-space learning opportunities where students can build their skills, hone their mindsets, and explore the connection between theory and practice. Across a student's academic journey,

Table 2.1   *The focus of our teaching: a guide for entrepreneurship educators*

Business basics	Entrepreneurship basics	Entrepreneurial mindset/ competencies
Setting up the books	Entrepreneurship defined	Opportunity alertness
How to sell	Entrepreneurial process	Risk mitigation
Hiring of staff	Characteristics of entrepreneurs	Resource leveraging
Forms of enterprise	Types of entrepreneurs	Conveying a compelling vision
Cash flow management	Contexts for entrepreneurship	Value innovation
Formulating strategy	Innovative business models	Passion
Market analysis	Entrepreneurial cognition	Persistence and tenacity
Setting up operations	Nature of opportunity	Creative problem-solving
Pricing	Opportunity discovery/creation	Guerrilla behavior
Promotion and advertising	Seed and venture capital	Optimism
Financial statements	Lean start-up	Learning from failure
Franchising	Entrepreneurial orientation	Implementing change
Management control	Entrepreneurship and society	Adaptation
Cost analysis	Ethical challenges in	Resilience
Protecting intellectual property	entrepreneurship	Building and using networks
Exit strategies		

Source: Adapted with permission from Morris and Liguori (2016).

it is a rare occurrence for one to find so many textbook topic areas interacting together within one organism (viz., the student-run venture). This is in part because, typically, a list of goals or objectives would be developed at the programmatic level for students (i.e., what are the key things students need to know and be able to do upon completion of this program), then individual courses would compartmentalize down from those goals to course-level objectives, with the assumption being the sum of all the parts (courses) will accomplish the programmatic goal (presumably to get students equipped enough to be effective in the real world). In entrepreneurship education we know two truths: (1) the secret sauce lies in the interconnectedness of the curricular and the co-curricular, and (2) we have reasonable consensus around what the focus of our teaching should be. With regard to the latter, Table 2.1 adapted from Morris and Liguori (2016) illustrates the three primary categories in which contemporary entrepreneurship education is focused, namely business basics, entrepreneurship basics, and entrepreneurial mindset and competencies.

In a traditional business school entrepreneurship degree program context, most faculty would presume the following with regard to these three categories:

• *Business Basics* are predominantly the dominion of the foundational core courses required for all business majors (accounting, finance, marketing, management, strategy, etc.). They are learned in the classroom through lectures, experiential exercises, textbooks, etc.

- *Entrepreneurship Basics* are predominantly the dominion of the core set of entrepreneurship courses required for the major (Entrepreneurship and Innovation, New Venture Development, Creativity and Innovation, etc.). They are learned in the classroom through lectures, experiential exercises, textbooks, etc.
- *Entrepreneurial Mindset / Competencies* are best learned by doing, by engaging in entrepreneurial action, by failure, and though persistence. These items, while talked about in class, are learned in practice. For these, having effective, engaging, and integrated co-curricular programming is key.

One could argue the statement "most faculty would presume" these three categories would be covered in this way is too bold, but let us offer two points of context. First, for the sake of understanding the big picture pieces of a very intricate puzzle, I'm talking in generalities. Second, many of the learning outcomes listed in the table will have multiple touch points which span the general business core, the entrepreneurship degree core, and co-curricular programming; this is as it should be.

Student-run ventures are uniquely positioned to bridge across these three domains and they provide opportunities for students to begin to build their entrepreneurial identities (cf. Duening & Metzger, 2017; Nielsen & Gartner, 2017). This will become apparent as you read the case narratives in the latter part of this book. In her chapter on Blue Connection Kate Flemming talks about students managing upwards of $50,000 in leveraged inventory, overseeing the marketing, promotion, and development of multiple events (business model innovation), experimenting with pricing models and calculating cost of goods sold, managing retail sales, operations and staffing, and seeking profit maximization. They are engaging as a middleman or platform connecting the community at large to the arts community. While doing all of these things, which span business basics and entrepreneurship basics, they are building and strengthening their entrepreneurial competencies and skillsets.

The same parallels come across when reading Dave Burdick's reflection on advising Art Circus. There, the students are tasked with creating culture as part of their value proposition, engaging in rapid prototyping and customer discovery, pricing tickets, recruiting sponsors, etc. All of these things have ties and root to business and entrepreneurship basics, but also help to develop mindset and competencies. Elements of risk and failure, persistence, resource leveraging, problem solving, and opportunity recognition, to name a few, get practiced.

REFERENCES

Baumol, W. J., & Strom, R. J. (2007). Entrepreneurship and economic growth. *Strategic Entrepreneurship Journal*, 1(1–2), 233–237.

Birch, D. L. (1987). *Job creation in America: How our smallest companies put the most people to work*. New York: The Free Press.

Duening, T. N., & Metzger, M. L. (Eds.). (2017). *Entrepreneurial identity: The process of becoming an entrepreneur*. Cheltenham, UK and Northampton, MA, USA: Edward Elgar Publishing.

Falk, J., & Alberti, F. (2000). The assessment of entrepreneurship education. *Industry and Higher Education*, 14(2), 101–108.

Greene, P. G., Katz, J. A., & Johannisson, B. (2004). Entrepreneurship education. *Academy of Management Learning & Education*, 3(3), 238–241.

Kassean, H., Vanevenhoven, J., Liguori, E., & Winkel, D. E. (2015). Entrepreneurship education: A need for reflection, real-world experience and action. *International Journal of Entrepreneurial Behavior & Research*, 21(5), 690–708.

Liguori, E., Corbin, R., Lackeus, M., & Solomon, S. J. (2019). Under-researched domains in entrepreneurship and enterprise education: Primary school, community colleges and vocational education and training programs. *Journal of Small Business and Enterprise Development*, 26(2), 182–189.

Morris, M. H., & Liguori, E. (2016). Preface: Teaching reason and the unreasonable. In M. H. Morris & E. Liguori (Eds.), *Annals of entrepreneurship education and pedagogy–2016*. Cheltenham, UK and Northampton, MA, USA: Edward Elgar Publishing.

Neck, H. M., & Greene, P. G. (2011). Entrepreneurship education: Known worlds and new frontiers. *Journal of Small Business Management*, 49(1), 55–70.

Neck, H. M., Greene, P. G., & Brush, C. G. (Eds.). (2014). *Teaching entrepreneurship: A practice-based approach*. Cheltenham, UK and Northampton, MA, USA: Edward Elgar Publishing.

Nielsen, S. L., & Gartner, W. B. (2017). Am I a student and/or entrepreneur? Multiple identities in student entrepreneurship. *Education + Training*, 59(2), 135–154.

Schumpeter, J. (1934). *Capitalism, socialism, and democracy*. New York: Harper & Row.

Stevenson, H. H., & Sahlman, S. (1986). Importance of entrepreneurship in economic development. In R. Hisrisch (Ed.), *Entrepreneurship, intrapreneurship and venture capital*. Lexington, KY: D. C. Heath.

Vanevenhoven, J., & Liguori, E. W. (2013). The impact of entrepreneurship education: Introducing the entrepreneurship education project. *Journal of Small Business Management*, 51(3), 315–328.

3. Creating a culture for student-run ventures

Julienne Shields

Exhilaration and frustration. Creative exploration and drudgery. Student-run ventures (SRVs) are a rare and challenging privilege to teach. The privilege, however, is in the unique way the experience shapes students who participate. Heidi Neck once said, "We've done our job if after taking an entrepreneurship course a student realizes he/she does not want to be an entrepreneur." This is especially the case within the context of facilitating and experiencing student-run ventures. The learning experience in SRVs is paramount.

Not all students immediately fall in love with student-run ventures. It is fairly common to get a traditionally-educated "good" student who struggles in an SRV course. They may struggle with customer interaction, lack empathy for clients and team members, get frustrated with a non-standard work schedule, have difficulty anticipating problems, refuse to accept responsibility, and just simply hate the experience. The uncertainty inherent in a student-run venture can paralyze some. Others thrive in the struggle and anguish. The students that thrive often enroll in multiple student-run ventures, think of new ways to combine resources, share learning with their peers, reach out to new customer groups, and research new ways of doing things on their own. Our philosophy is that both types of students can be entrepreneurs.

These are experiences that, at least within our context, cannot be mimicked by internships, a single semester-long project, or even a co-curricular project. Each of those mentioned above are important experiences in their own right, but their comparison is limited by their context.

As director of the Center for Entrepreneurship, it is a privilege to support student-run ventures, the faculty who facilitate and teach them, and the students who leverage the learning experiences inherent in them. Getting a clear picture in one's mind about what student-run ventures are and what they aren't can be challenging, yet it is essential. Millikin defines student-run ventures with the following criteria published in Kuratko, Cornwall and Morris' book *Entrepreneurship Programs and the Modern University* (2015):

- A laboratory of practice delivered as a course grounded in an academic discipline;
- Is student centered with faculty and practitioner coaching;
- Profit and mission-driven;
- A business operating in the marketplace where students are defining and designing the service and product offerings;
- And flexible so that students can experiment and adapt from semester to semester.

It is worth elaborating on Millikin's definition of SRVs to be clear and provide adequate context.

A laboratory of practice delivered as a course grounded in an academic discipline;

In SRVs, students conduct experiments. SRVs are a special kind of laboratory because activities are based in the practice of business – specifically with marketing, operations, finance, and within the discipline-specific industry in which they are grounded. Each laboratory is different, yet in some ways, interrelated.

One of the foundational components of a student-run venture is that it is indeed a "course." These are all credit-bearing courses, and that is an essential component. All have a faculty member assigned who are compensated for "teaching" the course. Students formally enroll in these classes, there is a syllabus with learning outcomes defined, milestones achieved, and grades earned.

Each year, fresh-eyed students will approach the Center for Entrepreneurship wanting to start a new SRV because they see the impressive things other students are doing in existing SRVs. Because they are not familiar with the definition, we educate them on the difference. They are surprised to find out that SRVs are classes, that they earn grades (and possibly money), but that they can't take the business with them when they leave. What they are really asking for is to start either a "student organization" or a "student-owned venture" (i.e., their own business) and those are great too, but they are not the same. SRVs have curriculum, learning objectives, faculty, etc. We consider it a testament to the programs that students want to imitate the SRVs, and we encourage students to create organizations as well as student-owned ventures.

Student centered with faculty and practitioner coaching;

Since there is a faculty assigned to the course, it might be tempting to assume that faculty is responsible for the business outcomes of the venture. This is mostly incorrect and is explained in greater detail in the best practices section of this book. Students are responsible for the business outcomes. They are at the center of the venture with a faculty member present for support – to serve as a mentor or coach for the students.

Profit and mission-driven;

From one semester to another, our SRVs are often not profitable. Does that mean we cannot say these laboratories are driven by profit? And why profit? Why not just revenue?

All SRVs focus on generating revenue, but students also need to consider expenses. This might seem like an obvious point, but when faculty or administration are looking to justify a venture based on profitability, it is essential to consider the importance of the learning that happens in both revenue generation and expense containment. We have continued to support the language "profit-driven" as appropriate as a result.

Mission-driven was also essential to include for the benefit of art students who were not interested so much in the word profit, but rather, drawn to mission-driven aspects of non-profits. Non-profits still need to earn enough money to pay the people leading and working in it, but the unfortunate perceived dichotomy between the words profit and non-profit lead students to believe that generating a profit (generating revenue and containing expenses) is not important or as important for non-profits.

Some individuals get hung up on a university saying that a classroom experience is "profit-driven" because academic institutions are by-and-large non-profit entities. Keep in mind that being profit-driven is a mindset, not a financial reality. And, being driven to make a profit is something that all for-profits and non-profits must do to justify their existence. The distinction of the definition is important, and after years of wrestling with this, we expect to revisit this with most new administrators to ensure they are comfortable with the concept.

Operating in the marketplace where students are defining and designing the service and product offerings;

A student-run venture is more than planning a one-time event in the semester. It is the difference between a bake sale and a bakery to use an oft-used phrase. Additionally, echoing the student-centered emphasis above, the students are the creative force behind responding to the resources they have and the needs in the market.

Flexible so that students can experiment and adapt from semester to semester.

This, in particular, is the part that causes critics to question if established student-run ventures are truly entrepreneurial endeavors. As the "business owner" vs. "entrepreneur" debate continues, we waste no time to advocate for developing competencies needed for starting and running a business using student-run ventures as the laboratory. The situation does warrant the use of acquisition entrepreneurship as a model since students are essentially acquiring the student-run venture once they enroll. Some ventures orient the new owners as having just acquired the business and now must navigate the work with an existing customer base, develop new customers, learn essential systems, and continue to generate revenue and make wise expense decisions.

Student-run ventures have no choice but to be flexible. Each semester comes with the risk of changing enrollment and a new team of actors within the business. This means that regardless of the design and structure of the SRV, there are always new elements within the laboratory of practice to leverage, develop, and mitigate.

Faculty members must also be flexible in their approach to teaching. Students will often trend toward making transactional decisions rather than thinking deeply about the consequences of their decisions. In this context, students may want to make a decision that has an effect on future semesters. This is not a bad thing, but it does require the facilitating faculty member to step in and discuss the consequences for the business, for future ownership teams, and the academic institution. When a competing landlord approaches students to offer a location with more promising foot traffic, which actually happened, students don't get the full authority to move to that new location. Situations like these result in throwing planned lessons out the window, and generate a rich and evocative dialogue.

The student-run venture is like a canvas. The student ownership team gets full authority to decide what paint or other materials are used on the canvas, what gets painted or put on the canvas, and if there are items that should be connected to the canvas and extend out from the canvas. But, their base is the canvas. Faculty provide the original frame, ensure that the canvas doesn't remain blank, and prevent the canvas from being set on fire.

The definition of a student-run venture raises several logistical questions. For example, How many student-run ventures do you have, and why?

The number of student-run ventures at Millikin changes from one year to the next. For years, the number of student-run ventures held steady at 5–6. Word started to spread about these ventures throughout campus, and so did the entrepreneurial bug. Faculty became very interested in innovating and creating new ventures. The number quickly jumped from 5 or 6 to 11. After reaching 11, it continued to increase to 15, which is how many SRVs we currently have. Student-run ventures, like businesses off-campus, come and go. Some have ended, others are still finding their footing, and others continue to grow year after year.

The breakdown of Millikin's 15 student-run ventures is as follows:

- 4 in music
- 5 in fine arts and design
- 3 in humanities (English, Spanish, and history)
- 1 in sports and exercise science
- 1 in information technology
- 1 shared by fine arts and humanities

The 15 student-run ventures are taught by 13 different faculty members, meaning two faculty members are pulling double-duty.

This book delves into the entrepreneurial endeavors on campus that are formally classified as student-run ventures as we define them. We will take a look at the following past and present student-run ventures:

- Pipe Dreams Studio Theatre
- Arts Circus
- Blue Satellite Press
- Blue Connection Retail Art Gallery
- Arts Café
- MUPC (Millikin University Performance Consulting)

Each of these student-run ventures is unique in their application of teaching entrepreneurial competencies and skills. They have their own creation story, history, industry-specific discipline, local market, respective marketing channels, team structure, level of consistency, and challenges.

Before getting to the challenges and how faculty can mentor students through them when they appear, discussed in the best practices chapter, we will start with our start – the history of SRVs at Millikin. We will then move on to discuss faculty, profitability, and failure before diving into each of the six case studies.

HISTORY

The first student-run venture at Millikin was the music recording label First Step Records, formed in 1999. It was driven from the School of Music and not mainly involved with the Center for Entrepreneurship, which was just beginning at the time. The following year, professors Sharon Alpi (entrepreneurship), Dr. Rick Bibb (marketing), and Ed Walker (art) started working with a handful of business students to create a feasibility study on a retail art gallery that would become the Blue Connection student-run venture.

Table 3.1 Student-run ventures at Millikin University (as of 3/1/2020)

	Students are typically from these major/programs	Laboratory is presented as a Profit or Non-profit	MU Owned/ Rent Space	On/Off Campus	Credits	Student Enrollment	Typical Semesters	Faculty	Year started	Year ended	Required in major
First Step Records	Music business	Profit	Owned	On	1	8–15	2–4	1	2001		N
Blue Connection	Studio art, business, communication	Profit	Rent	Off	1–3	8–18	1	1–2	2002		Y
Bronze Man Books	English, publishing, graphic design	Profit	Owned	On	1–3	10–15	2–4	2	2006	2019	N
Blue Satellite Press	English, art, graphic design	Profit	Owned	Adjacent	1	5–8	1–2	1	2009		N
Carriage House Press	Art	Profit	Owned	Off	1	4–8	1–2	1	2009		N
Pipe Dreams Studio Theatre	Theatre (all majors)	Non-profit	Owned	Adjacent	1	12–18	3–6	1	2010		N
Ignite Studios	Graphic design	Profit	Owned	On	3	6–12	1	1	2013		N
Art Circus	Music business, theatre	Profit	Owned	On	1	5–8	1–2	1	2015	2016	N
MUPC (MU Performance Consulting)	Information systems, business	Profit	Owned	Adjacent/ Owned	1	8–12	1–4	1	2015		N

	Students are typically from these major/programs	Laboratory is presented as a Profit or Non-profit	MU Owned/ Rent Space	On/Off Campus	Credits	Student Enrollment	Typical Semesters	Faculty	Year started	Year ended	Required in major
Big Blue Personal Training	Physical training, health-related	Profit	Owned	On	1	3–4	1	1	2015	on hold	N
MARS (Millikin Audio Recording Studios)	Music business, commercial music	Profit	Owned	On	1	5–8	1–3	1	2016		N
MIST (Music Industry Study Tours)	Music business, commercial music	Profit	Owned	On	1–3	8–12	1–2	1	2016		N
Clio Consulting	History, political science	Profit	Owned	On	1	5–8	on hold	1	2017	on hold	N
Arts Café	Music, music business	Profit	Owned	On	1	8–15	1–3	1	2017		N
Blue Brew	Entrepreneurship, marketing	Profit	Rent	Off	1–3	10–16	1–3	2	2017		N
Millikin Creates	Graphic design, communications	Profit	Owned	On	1–3	6–12	1–3	1	2018		?
Mosaicos	Spanish, journalism	In progress									

Table 3.1 is a list of all current ventures with the date they began, and other features we consider as we look at student-run venture configurations. This serves as a snapshot in time of the landscape of student-run ventures at an institution, as I can guarantee that this list will continue to change. These ventures are intended to shift and change with the environment and available resources organically.

THE ENTREPRENEURIAL FACULTY MEMBER

Being a faculty member responsible for a student-run venture is challenging. There is consistently a balance between owning the experience of the course and owning the actual output of the work the students are creating in the venture. Too loose of a grip on the course itself and the intentionality of the learning objectives is lost. Too tight of a grip and the students start behaving more like employees and miss intended learning objectives. The balance of this will be determined by trial and error and critical reflection.

Some questions faculty are encouraged to ask themselves are:

- What would failure look like to me, and what would failure look like with regard to learning outcomes? What is the difference between the two?
- How did I handle it when students started to make decisions that might not lead to a successful outcome?
- How many decisions did I make for the students?
- Were students actively recruiting other students for the next semester? If not, why? If so, how?
- How were the students' individual strengths leveraged to impact the venture, and were they knowingly doing so?
- Were there processes that needed to be modified? Can the process be modified in between semesters or can/could the modifications be a part of the learning objectives next semester?
- How was failure presented, received, avoided, anticipated, celebrated?
- Was the space used for class meetings the same or different than where the venture functions? How might this have impacted the overall objectives of the course?

These are just a few of the questions faculty ask themselves, and by-and-large, these are interesting and probing questions that elevate the autonomy of a faculty member. There is a sense of both intimacy and detachment that exists in this process. From my own experience, being busy with work outside the teaching of the student-run venture helps facilitate this balance. There is only so much I could control, and the rest I needed to let go and truly allow students to handle. There were times I was incredibly pleased with the results, and other times that I was embarrassed for them. However, learning occurred regardless of the outcome.

FACULTY PREPARATION

Faculty preparation is a major element for success in SRVs, although a faculty member overseeing an SRV may never truly feel "prepared." Over the years, the primary introduction infusing entrepreneurship into the curriculum has been through the faculty development with the Coleman Foundation Fellows program. We also sent all entrepreneurship fellows and business faculty to the Experiential Classroom. It proved to be an excellent way to start the conversation of how engaging classrooms can be when infusing entrepreneurial components into the curriculum.

On campus, there are also professional development programs and workshop series available to faculty. Conferences that focus on entrepreneurship pedagogy such as USASBE's annual conference and discipline-specific conferences that accepted topics on entrepreneurship are also excellent resources for faculty to develop and prepare their courses. The Center consistently supports and shares ideas, but faculty have the autonomy to develop their course proactively and independently. Often, the best thing the Center provides is an ear and sounding board, which is also what faculty members should provide to students in an SRV.

There is no single profile for learning tools, but the Center recommends to faculty a variety of frameworks and pedagogical supports within a loose "toolkit."

- Business Model Canvas
- FOCUS Framework (Justin Wilcox)
- Competencies model (Morris)
- Lean Canvas
- Budget spreadsheet
- Agile orientation
- Facilitation skills

There are other factors related to general business knowledge that are important. As a general rule, it is important for faculty to be well-versed in the difference between for-profit business models and non-profit business models, or at least the difference between the two. While most SRVs that offer course credit are going to be non-profit technically, they are presented to students as for-profit businesses. Students can be tempted to be comfortable just covering expenses, and while the university or institution may be ok with that, it does not elevate the competitive and entrepreneurial spirit. It sets the bar particularly low – especially since many SRVs are already subsidized in some form or another by the university.

All the preparation in the world doesn't truly prepare a faculty member for what happens the moment a student-run venture is launched. Just as in launching a startup, planning is one thing, but being flexible to reality is more important than preparation on its own.

COURSE DESIGNS

As discussed in this book, there are as many different kinds of student-run ventures as there are faculty who teach them. Designing courses that are effective require an instructor to go back to the beginning and look at the fundamentals. Faculty ask the following questions among others when starting and overseeing an SRV:

1. How will this experience develop entrepreneurial skills and, ultimately, competencies?
2. How is the experience articulated in the learning outcomes?
3. How will this course showcase my strengths as a faculty member, or am I looking to work on challenges that I may have as an entrepreneurial instructor?
4. Who are the partners being engaged with this venture, and will that change from one semester to another?
5. Are there written agreements needed prior to student engagement so the instructor's intended design is upheld?
6. What kind of communication and document repository tools are ready for use? Is there a requirement to use academic tools like Canvas or Blackboard, or can more professional tools like Dropbox, Drive, or Basecamp be used?
7. Are there events? If so, how many? One is likely too few, but what is the max?
8. Is the course a multiple-semester, leadership development design? Or is it a "drink from a firehose" one-semester experience?
9. Will there be extensive use of teams for accountability? Or just partners?

As you will learn, being thoughtful in the design upfront is clearly appropriate. Talking with faculty familiar with organizational design, entrepreneurship, and management can help, and bringing in examples from actual professional businesses and how they are structured is also highly advantageous. Their experience is good, but they must be cautious not to mimic it precisely as their resources, partners, cashflow, etc. are distinctly different than a student-run venture.

Student leadership in a venture is also an interesting opportunity for course design. Will the faculty select the leaders? It will be efficient, but what if the faculty chooses someone who has challenging interactions with his or her peers? Will leaders naturally emerge within a venture without faculty intervention? Definitely, but that might take precious time away and be a rocky process. Will students interview and select leaders for the subsequent semester? This can work well, but it can become a popularity contest, and what happens if a student must withdraw from the experience or even institution? Leadership is one of those tricky and important determinations in the course design. Again, there is no "right" way to do it, but being thoughtful about this is an important factor.

PROFITABILITY

You may be thinking, "Are your ventures profitable?" You will have a clear answer after reading about our ventures in the chapters to follow, but in short, no! Changing the entire ownership team every 4–6 months is not a formula for a successful business. Also, earning a profit within student-run ventures is not the point. Seeking to make a profit, however, is the point. Frankly, even the ventures that claim to be profitable are not including all the overhead costs in their projections. But this shouldn't determine success. A college chemistry lab isn't successful because it is profitable. It is successful by the learning that transpires within it. This is the attitude institutions should have when considering to bring SRVs onto campus.

To further the chemistry laboratory analogy, sometimes in a chemistry experiment, the various stages are broken down step by step to be tried and retried for consistency or variance. That is similar to what we do with the finances in student-run ventures. Students are not in charge of a large majority of the venture, but not "soup to nuts." For example, students can certainly make decisions on marketing expenses, certain operating expenses, revenue-generating events and promotions, customer service training, etc., but they don't often get to choose a site location with a particular rent or the state of the finances when they enroll in the SRV. Some things they work with and can control and others they cannot. The faculty's job is to thoughtfully determine what extent of control the students have and then lead students through a discussion about profitability goals for the semester or year.

ROLE OF FAILURE

The reality is that the only kind of failure in SRVs is inaction. Rather than the "Do or do not; there is no try," coined by Jedi-master Yoda, for students in a student-run venture, it may be more apt to say "Try or do; there is no do not."

Action is the currency of the land in student-run ventures. When students act and fail, this is a cause for celebration. We learned something through action, great! And yet some great opportunities for learning come from when something was totally dropped, and embarrassment ensued. This kind of failure – inactive failure – is often not celebrated, but is leveraged as an opportunity by faculty to draw out desired learning outcomes. We will come back to the role of failure as a faculty member in the final chapter of this book along with other best practices that prepare you to move forward after reading about six of our SRVs.

SETTING THE STAGE

Getting students to begin thinking about their role in a SRV as an owner and not as a passive course enrollee takes some work. To help set the stage before the semester even begins, below is a draft open letter to students which you have permission to use, adopt, and/or edit however convenient.

Open Letter to Students

Dear Owner,

Congratulations! You are now an owner of the [*name of venture*] student-run venture (SRV) here at [*name of institution*]. In this student-run venture course, you will be referred to not as a student, but as an owner. You, while working with your peers, will determine the success or failure of this venture.

I am not your teacher in this course; there is no teacher. My role, as faculty advisor of this venture, is to serve as a mentor, feedback facilitator, partner, and opportunity creator.

This letter is to welcome you on this journey, while detailing my expectations and your responsibilities.

My Expectations

I expect you not to "fail." You will have ideas, campaigns, products, events, and/or services that will fail, but the only true form of failure in an SRV is failure to act. I expect that you will be a dedicated and hard-working owner of this venture, and will accept nothing less.

You enrolled in this course, now I ask that you make the most of it. To make the most of this experience, you must commit yourself to it. You must go "all-in" and hold nothing back. Based on my exposure and the exposure my peers have had to student-run ventures, student owners who give it their all do not regret this experience; they thrive from it.

Running a business is hard. Entrepreneurs often have stressful lives. This course will not be easy, as it is intended to give you an authentic entrepreneurial experience. You will work hard and be uncomfortable. Over time, you will begin to get comfortable being uncomfortable.

I expect you to accept that you cannot control every aspect of this venture, but as part of the ownership team, take responsibility for the results your team produces. Accept the results of each activity, reflect, and make necessary changes to improve future results. By doing this, you will learn, have fun, and hopefully, set [*insert venture name here*] up for success and keep it going, leaving a legacy behind that future students can build upon.

In this SRV course, you are responsible for the following:

- Engaging in the Process
- Accepting Feedback
- Being Vulnerable
- Embracing Mistakes
- Taking Action

It is time to start your entrepreneurial journey. I hope you are excited, committed, and ready to get to work. After all, you now "own" this business.

I look forward to meeting and learning along with you on [*insert first day of class date here*].

Sincerely,

Professor [*insert name*]
Faculty Advisor

CONCLUSION

I believe the stories we are going to explore in this book are powerful. Student-run ventures – for our university and possibly yours – are powerful. They are an impactful way to teach and to learn for both faculty and students. In addition to the traditional "faculty teach and student learn" modality, faculty learn something new each semester. Faculty also learn from their students, and these students will have opportunities to teach their peers, and carry these lessons with them as they start their own businesses, join startups, work for corporations, or experiment with alternative career paths.

Student-run ventures are entrepreneurial laboratories. They are forced and not always successful from a financial sense. However, the skills and competencies built are genuine. Students learn creative problem solving, self-efficacy, proactiveness, optimism, articulating a vision, and more. Isn't that worth exploring?

4. Role clarity in SRVs: students, faculty, and administrators

Julienne Shields, Eric W. Liguori, and Mark Tonelli

One of the most critical aspects of a student-run venture is the need for very clear roles. Faculty leadership micromanaging the SRV, students not developing an owner's mindset, and administration not making learning the primary focus, are indicators your SRV is not living up to its potential in terms of being a high-impact learning opportunity for students. These things are also common symptoms of an SRV that does not have understandable, defined roles for each actor involved in the process. Thus, this chapter aims to provide a plausible framework for facilitating role clarity in SRVs, so that they can truly be run in the most impactful way possible for students. The three primary roles in an SRV are administration, faculty, and students. A true student-run venture needs all three involved, engaged, and open to working together to yield desired results.

Table 4.1 categorizes the key roles by actor, each of which is then discussed in more detail.

ROLE OF ADMINISTRATION

Administrators play an important role in SRVs given they typically are the individuals approving and funding the venture. Successful SRVs are a strategically integrated part of a university, and for that to happen, the administration must play an active role. At Millikin, the administration is supportive, and understands that new SRVs will form and existing SRVs will fail. They accept the ups and downs that come with SRVs, which can be costly and risky. These costs and risks must be balanced with the rewards of having unique and differentiated programs.

A commitment to a student-run venture is a commitment to an experience. And the experience is what faculty focus on as well. One example discussed later in this book is Art Circus, a dynamic venture that focused on creating multi-disciplinary art experiences at unique and disparate venues. After one year, the faculty lead was able to say, "this isn't working as anticipated," and

Table 4.1   *Administrator, faculty, and student roles*

Actor	Role summary
Administration	Empower faculty
	Create opportunities and provide resources
	Remove hurdles
	Make connections
	Navigate bureaucracy
Faculty	Mentor
	Facilitate feedback
	Partner with administration
	Create opportunities
	Provide continuity
	Offer context on the past
	Make students owners
Students	Engage sincerely
	Accept feedback
	Be vulnerable
	Embrace failure
	Do the work

pivoted and rebranded the experience to a new venture with more student buy-in. No one questioned his decision, and in fact, his willingness to admit that it wasn't working was honored and celebrated.

Ideally, the administration should empower faculty, create opportunities and provide resources, remove hurdles, make connections, and navigate bureaucracy.

Empower Faculty

Although students may expect them to, faculty members overseeing SRVs will not have all the answers. The 13 faculty members at Millikin overseeing our 15 SRVs come from different backgrounds and have different levels of expertise in business. They also have differing access to resources. They don't need to be experts because they are surrounded with the support they need.

The primary role of the administration is to give faculty what they need to allow students to come away with an authentic and beneficial learning experience. Administration helps fill in the gaps for each SRV by serving as the support system to each faculty member. This is not as burdensome as it may appear, but there are requirements up front to put a system in place that will support SRVs and allow faculty to take this system and run with it when starting a new venture with students.

Create Opportunities and Provide Resources

Using an analogy from Sarasvathy (2009) and subsequent conceptualization by Neck, Greene, and Brush (2014), think about roles in terms of puzzles and quilts. Student-run ventures are essentially assembled by patchwork, not puzzling. Administrators should shy away from puzzle-type approaches; they should not say here is the exact picture they want replicated and here are all the pieces, and then expect faculty to supervise students in assembly of a perfect image. Instead, administrators should think of their role as helping set a general overarching vision for what could be (big picture), and then providing "patches of fabric" in the form of resources and opportunities which students can begin to assemble together, or disregard. Entrepreneurship is analogous to quilting; administrators focus on the bigger picture goals, they assemble resources imperfectly, and often things don't fit together with puzzle-like precision.

Administrators can take two approaches to providing "patches of fabric": (1) be reactive, responding to and meeting requests made by faculty and students, or (2) be proactive, advocating on behalf of SRVs and creating puzzle pieces that may not be needed yet.

Both are helpful, but being proactive has the most significant positive impact on a university and a student-run venture. For example, let's say your institution shares a city with a large insurance company, and you have a working relationship with them. At a rotary meeting or networking event, a member of your administration shares information about your SRVs with the local business community. One of the executives of the insurance company approaches this member of your administration, and explains that they were planning on outsourcing their new coffee shop that was created in their headquarters, but may now consider allowing it to become an SRV. This may turn out to be a dud, but the opportunity was created by a proactive administration.

Administrations can also be proactive within their institution – recognizing opportunities on campus for faculty and staff to explore. Does your institution pay local companies to complete services on campus? Would any of these services be able to be completed by students in an SRV? Although the administration at your school can't successfully put an SRV together on their own, they can offer up or help provide access to these kinds of opportunities and the key resources needed for an SRV to manifest.

Remove Hurdles

There are many forms of hurdles that SRVs must overcome, and most of them will require intervention from the administration. Student-run ventures collect revenue. Revenue comes with responsibilities, from charging sales tax to deciding how this money will flow through the university. There will need to be buy-in from several different departments, and at first, many of them will either want to say no or implement restrictive boundaries that make operating an SRV nearly impossible. Removing this hurdle takes buy-in from the administration.

Not every business complies with standard academic periods. An administration must help triage issues, from allowing SRV courses to operate slightly outside the bounds of a normal course to simplifying purchase contracts and other necessary parts of operating an SRV. Like all businesses, SRVs face hurdles, and an administration, not faculty alone, are responsible for leading the charge past these hurdles.

Make Connections

Administrators are involved at different levels on campus. At one university, they may be proactively paving the way for multiple SRVs to exist and thrive, and at others, they may simply be willing to make connections. Administrations can facilitate connections and partnerships between SRVs, local businesses, faculty, members of the community, etc. Being open to making these connections provides support to faculty and students while creating a clear and beneficial channel where students and the faculty member overseeing an SRV can ask for help, and the administration will make connections that will fill that need.

Navigate Bureaucracy

Mixing academics with business gets messy. Students, and sometimes, even faculty, don't understand the administrative side of things, from taxes and tax ID numbers to following specifications for point of sale systems. Regardless of a group of students' enthusiasm going into the start of an SRV, students can't properly navigate the bureaucracy that's present at every university; but the administration can.

Want to host a live performance on campus? Well, what do you know about insurance riders for artists? Understandably, students have yet to gain exposure to these types of issues, but an administrator can help them navigate these potential problems, and by working closely with faculty members, train students to ask the right questions.

ROLE OF FACULTY

A faculty member leads each SRV course, which makes it tempting to assume that they are responsible for the business outcomes of a venture. This is mostly incorrect. Faculty members work with administrators to build the structure and implement the rules, and then empower students to take over the venture. Students are ultimately responsible for the business outcomes of a venture. The overseeing faculty member is responsible for the learning outcomes of the venture and fidelity to the financial responsibilities for reporting revenue and sales tax to the business office (students can be assigned to do this, but the faculty are responsible for ensuring it gets done at Millikin).

As administrators empower faculty, faculty members are responsible for empowering students. Ideally, faculty does the following for students: mentor, facilitate feedback, partner with administration, create opportunities, provide continuity, offer context on the past, and make students owners of the business.

Mentor

The role a faculty member plays in an SRV is foreign to many educators. Faculty are not in charge of making decisions, but they assume the position of a mentor. As a mentor, faculty should provide expertise and guidance without forcing the hand of students. The role a faculty member plays in an SRV can also be compared to a lifeguard. As a lifeguard, you want to guide and watch over swimmers, but you can't take strokes for them. Some of the best learning experiences might come from sinking to the bottom for a moment. But unlike a lifeguard, sometimes mentors have to watch a venture drown without taking on the full responsibility of bringing it back to the surface. No one, from the students to faculty to administrators, wants a venture to fail, but failure can't always, and shouldn't always, be avoided at all costs.

Additionally, while mentors are actively watching, it is also important to note that they are not actively walking the paths the students are walking. Humility is incredibly important for the mentor as they are providing expertise and guidance. A faculty member at another institution expressed significant frustration that his students were not taking his hard-earned advice honed over the course of his career. That was the A-ha moment. He was in his late twenties when he even started to learn about the issue he was trying to get them to master (which he did not master until later). In some ways, just making them aware of it in their early twenties may be the great gift he gave to them, even if they did not choose to master dealing with the issue.

Facilitate Feedback

As mentors, faculty must facilitate feedback from students – feedback on the venture, structure, peers, support from administration, and the course. By sharing feedback and having their opinion considered and acted upon when necessary, students are empowered like the owners of a business, who can make decisions for their company as they see fit. An open line of communication and trust (both ways) is essential to facilitate feedback from students.

Partner with Administration

Administration and faculty must be on the same page. They don't have to agree on every decision, nor should they, but if they are at odds, the venture and students suffer as a result. At Millikin, administration understands and supports the mission of each SRV, and this partnership allows faculty and students to experiment, succeed, and fail.

Create Opportunities

Faculty each have unique networks, backgrounds, and areas of expertise. This results in a unique base to draw on when creating opportunities for an SRV. Faculty members are often also business owners, consultants, members of local boards, and valued members of the community with ties to organizations. They can use these relationships to bring new opportunities to students. Faculty also control the curriculum and are responsible for getting the course to count for credit. If structured properly, the course can result in credit and the opportunity to earn money for students, which is more desirable than just one or the other.

Provide Continuity

Students change from one semester to the next in an SRV, but faculty can provide continuity – keeping the venture going despite constant turnover. For example, some semesters may hit SRVs harder than others, requiring more guidance from faculty. Unfortunately, when you have a strong year with solid student leadership, the following year or semester tends to be weaker because of the level of management and control the previous team had. Succession must be made a priority in these instances, and it is the responsibility of faculty to anticipate declines in leadership and recommend that student leaders put a strong succession plan into place and mentor future leaders of the venture.

As faculty, you want students to build systems and handbooks that allow the venture to be handed down from generation to generation, but you will have to guide them towards this decision. Faculty are also responsible for making sure this information is passed down since leadership groups are unlikely to meet their successors. And frankly, even with a handbook, some semesters the students will choose to start over from scratch – because entrepreneurs will need to create their own playbook.

Offer Context on the Past

Providing continuity may require offering context on the past. Students are unlikely to know the history of the venture, what has and hasn't worked in the past, what events have been hosted or products have been sold. Faculty may choose to share this information. Offering context on the past also comes into play when mentoring without making decisions for the venture. But be careful when sharing historical information. There is risk of being seen as out-of-touch and controlling, and this is a major concern. Balance historical context with considerations for how it might have worked under different conditions. You don't want to make the final say when it comes to an important decision for the venture, and you can provide unique insight and share the experiences of previous student leadership groups.

Make Students Owners

All student-run ventures are backed by Millikin and are not stand-alone enterprises. That said, being under the umbrella of Millikin is intentionally under-emphasized with students. Among faculty who teach student-run ventures, there is an understanding that there is a degree of "theatre" required to help students embrace an ownership mentality to think, feel, and act like they are the owners of a student-run venture. We do not avoid the realities, but we are careful to use language that supports their ownership of effort. For example, we do not refer to students who enroll in the ventures as "Blue Connection students" or "Blue Brew students" but rather, "ownership team" or "leadership team." And with those who spearhead the launch of a student-run venture, we call them the "founders." The language we use to refer to students who enroll in the classes shapes and reinforces their perceptions of themselves.

The real owner of a student-run venture is not the students; it's the university. However, students take ownership each year or semester and must be empowered to feel that this is their own business. Without this feeling, students will fail to gain an authentic entrepreneurial experience and will not be "all-in." Feeling that there is no true ownership for students comes from how the faculty member crafts the environment. Faculty must carefully approach how they get students to believe that they own the business.

ROLE OF STUDENTS

As with every course, an SRV needs students. But students can't just show up – they have responsibilities and important roles to play that extend far beyond what they have in a traditional course. Explained above, students are responsible for the business outcomes of a venture. They identify inventory and service offerings, articulate the value of their products and services, and initiate contractual relationships. Ventures are decidedly student-centered endeavors. They must take risks and experience the rewards. In an SRV, in addition to business outcomes, students are responsible for engaging sincerely, accepting feedback, being vulnerable, and embracing failure.

Engage Sincerely

Taking a course on management requires studying and paying attention, but it doesn't require a sincere level of engagement and buy-in. Businesses thrive when their employees are actively engaged and passionate in their roles and the company. The same can be said with an SRV. Many SRVs are not courses that are open to all students, nor should they be. A student needs to have an active interest in the SRV and interest in learning while working inside a business to have an optimal experience. Ventures fail without proper inputs. If a student isn't in it to win it and all-in, it will be difficult for them to put in what is needed for the SRV to thrive and for the student to take away desired learning outcomes.

Accept Feedback

SRVs are organized to facilitate feedback. Feedback can come at students from all directions – students, faculty, administration, customers, partners, mentors, and others. Students are responsible for accepting feedback and utilizing that feedback to iterate. Accepting feedback does not require a student to use that feedback, as they must decide what feedback to take to heart and what feedback is not useful at that time, but it does require that they keep an open mind and seek feedback from others.

Be Vulnerable

For leadership positions in an SRV, feedback and vulnerability go hand in hand. This is similar to what occurs within the role of a manager in a business off campus. Peers may question their decisions, talk behind their backs, and try to take over their roles. All students in an SRV must be vulnerable and open, which allows for additional learning opportunities, and to grow within their position in the SRV. The more they can grow in their role, the more ready they will be for future leadership positions.

Embrace Failure

Failure in an SRV is a learning opportunity. To be clear, the only real "failure" in an SRV is inaction. However, students, as "owners" of the venture, see failure differently than administration and faculty. From failure, whether a sparsely attended event, a losing quarter, or the end of the venture, students learn about marketing, business finance, public relations, and much more. In an SRV, things will hardly ever go as expected. Accepting that reality is vital for learning. Students don't have to necessarily embrace or celebrate failure, but they need to accept the reality of the situation, whatever that may be, and practice deep reflection. Deep reflection should focus on successes, failures, and what was learned along the way. Without it, misconceptions are likely, and students might have a skewed perception of why an activity or process succeeded or failed. As long as students are open to accepting reality and practicing deep reflection, they will learn from the SRV, and to a level that is not possible in other courses.

Do the Work

Ideas are easy, execution is hard, and it is often those who execute who come out ahead. There is not much room for shortcuts in running a successful venture. Like most aspiring entrepreneurs, students tend to overvalue ideas and underestimate the amount of work it will take to successfully execute on those ideas. Students need to be prepared to put in more hours when engaging with an SRV than they would in most any other more traditional academic course.

CONCLUSION

While at the end of the day role clarity is critical, fuzzy lines always exist. Given the majority of work in the venture is done at the student and faculty levels, this is where the most challenges often arise. We suggest both faculty and students keep Table 4.2 handy, so as day-to-day questions arise there is a clear reference for where responsibility lies.

Every time student and/or faculty leadership change within the venture there is an inherent period of calibration needed. Students need to figure out how to work collaboratively to move the venture forward, how to take control and develop their owners' mindsets. Similarly, faculty need to gain a sense of comfort and trust with the student leadership team so they can better resist the temptation to overstep and/or micromanage. They also need to continue to recognize that failure is inherent, so while sometimes painful to watch, students need to be allowed to fail as we learn from failure. In this sense, faculty's role then is to not prevent failure, but to guide the students through debriefing

Table 4.2   *Faculty and student responsibilities*

Responsibilities	Faculty	Students
Identifying learning outcomes	X	
Creating a budget		X
Identifying clients	By association/networks	Primarily responsible
Drafting contracts		X
Signing contracts	Primarily responsible	Possibly, depending on the situation
Signing checks/approving payments	Primarily responsible	
Ordering supplies		Primarily responsible
Writing checks, not signing		Primarily responsible
Organizing the work		Primarily responsible
Creating marketing messages	Reviewing	Primarily responsible
Identifying and testing marketing channels		Primarily responsible
Reporting monthly financials		Primarily responsible
Creating annual financials	Possibly responsible	Primarily responsible
Submitting annual financials to Business Office	Primarily responsible	

failure and practicing deep reflection, arguably the most valuable part of the student's learning process (cf. Gartner, Stam, Thompson, & Verduyn, 2016; Kassean, Vanevenhoven, Liguori, & Winkel, 2015; Neck & Corbett, 2018; Neck, Greene, & Brush, 2014).

REFERENCES

Gartner, W. B., Stam, E., Thompson, N., & Verduyn, K. (2016). Entrepreneurship as practice: Grounding contemporary practice theory into entrepreneurship studies. *Entrepreneurship and Regional Development*, 28(9–10), 813–816.

Kassean, H., Vanevenhoven, J., Liguori, E., & Winkel, D. E. (2015). Entrepreneurship education: A need for reflection, real-world experience and action. *International Journal of Entrepreneurial Behavior & Research*, 21(5), 690–708.

Neck, H. M., & Corbett, A. C. (2018). The scholarship of teaching and learning entrepreneurship. *Entrepreneurship Education and Pedagogy*, 1(1), 8–41.

Neck, H. M., Greene, P. G., & Brush, C. G. (Eds.). (2014). *Teaching entrepreneurship: A practice-based approach.* Cheltenham, UK and Northampton, MA, USA: Edward Elgar Publishing.

Sarasvathy, S. D. (2009). *Effectuation: Elements of entrepreneurial expertise.* Cheltenham, UK and Northampton, MA, USA: Edward Elgar Publishing.

5. Student-run venture outcomes

Julienne Shields and Mark Tonelli

Student-run ventures are unique, yet the experiences of and lessons learned by students who participate in SRVs are often similar. In Arts Circus, students organized one-of-a-kind events that brought different types of performances and performers together. In the Blue Connection Art Gallery SRV, which is still active, students operate an off-campus art gallery. Both are very different, yet students involved in each are put in situations where they are encouraged to plan, lead, sell (tickets/art), market, network, and iterate along the way.

All SRVs under the umbrella of an institution, regardless of their focus or structure, likely have shared target outcomes. These target outcomes shape the ventures and the experiences of students. So what are the target outcomes of a profit-driven student-run venture? While the answer may seem obvious, not all outcomes are financial. SRVs don't typically make a profit, nor is that the primary goal.

Setting target outcomes at your institution will be the responsibility of faculty and administrators, and these outcomes need to align with the desires of administration. Whatever outcomes are chosen, focus should not be lost on learning outcomes being the key deliverable of an SRV. At Millikin, there is no pressure placed on ventures to generate a profit, nor is losing money frowned upon. Instead, we divide outcomes into two categories: university outcomes and student outcomes.

UNIVERSITY OUTCOMES

Prior to an SRV opening for enrollment, target outcomes for the university should be set. An institution has much to gain from an SRV, but without setting these goals, the purpose of launching and running SRVs can easily get lost. Common target outcomes for universities include publicity, prestige, resume and employability, engagement with students and community, and enrollment.

Publicity

Publicity is a key target outcome for many institutions that support SRVs. From podcast appearances to local news stories to television coverage to this

35

book, SRVs are perfect for media coverage and ripe with sharable positive stories that are attractive and informative to the local community, prospective students, faculty, local businesses, and others. Not only can we promote our university through student-run ventures, but we have also been promoting entrepreneurship and student-run ventures to the world, which means our impact at Millikin is spreading beyond Decatur, Illinois.

Publicity initiatives focused on SRVs benefit institutions, ventures, and students by bringing awareness to these ventures throughout the community. While failure is common, and there is some possibility of negative PR coverage, the chances of negative press are low, and the amount of positive media attention we've received has far outweighed any negative effects of a student-run venture closing here at Millikin.

Setting publicity as a target outcome at the start of launching your first SRV can open additional doors for students and the university. Podcasts, newsletters, virtual documentaries, vlogs, and blogs are all attractive outlets that can feature information about your SRVs, and can also be created internally to promote your efforts.

Prestige

Student-run ventures bring a level of prestige to overseeing faculty, participating students, and the university. Prestige can be used as a recruitment tool, attracting students to a venture, and attracting faculty and students to the institution. SRVs can also raise the profile of your university nationwide through PR efforts, mentioned above.

Setting prestige as a target outcome of SRVs can be tricky, as you will need to carefully weigh the benefits with the risks of heavily relying on the number of ventures and the level of success of each. Ventures succeed and fail, and your university should ensure that while using SRVs to build prestige, it also stresses that learning outcomes are key. Neither monetary success nor longevity of a particular venture should be overly emphasized in PR efforts or building prestige due to supporting SRVs.

Resume and Employability

Producing employable graduates is a goal of every university, and should be a desired target outcome of your SRV program. Student-run ventures provide a perfect opportunity for students to bolster resumes, build credibility and experience, and gain the attention and respect of their future employers. Self-employment is also possible for those who have worked in SRVs, and at an increased rate based on our observations.

Setting resumes and employability as a target outcome will help guide your SRVs to have more defined roles and track results and activities. This information provides a way to measure results, and for students to share their experiences with others, including employers.

Engagement with Students and Community

Student-run ventures change the traditional roles of teachers and students. The faculty in a course are not responsible for the success or failure of the course as it relates to the venture. Faculty serve as both mentors and peers who learn along with their students each semester.

We have witnessed an unmatched level of engagement in SRVs, and students and faculty form strong bonds during the process. The bonds created between faculty and students are similar to the bonds formed among peers who are working together to grow a business – because that's what they are doing! Student-run ventures not only bring students and faculty closer together, but they also connect the university and students to the community, especially in SRVs that operate off campus like the Blue Connection Art Gallery. Having an SRV out in the community raises awareness to these ventures and your institution's activities.

Enrollment

Every team, from a basketball roster to a group of employees in a business, needs a specific number of people to play necessary roles. All ventures have needs when it comes to the number of students enrolled in the venture, and some ventures have specific target enrollment outcomes. These outcomes must make logistical sense for the business. Too few students, and the business cannot function without intervention. An excess of students in an SRV, and students without clear responsibilities and tasks could impact morale and their peers in a negative way.

To ensure enough students are enrolling in an SRV, recruitment is essential. Both faculty and students recruit others to join an SRV. However, students are much more effective at recruiting their peers, and should be encouraged to lead recruitment efforts over time. Recruiting methods are both active and passive, and include:

- One-on-one networking events or opportunities
- Marketing throughout campus
- Student organized SRV fairs
- Interviews required to "make" it into a venture
- Poaching from other ventures

Recruiting methods mentioned above are active recruitment methods. Passive recruiting is based on the commentary of students – how they feel about the venture as they are going about their daily activities. If they are complaining about tasks or the venture as a whole, this impacts the perception their peers have about their experience. The quality of the work and the product is also a form of passive recruitment for student-run ventures. If students perceive that there is pride in the experience, they want to be a part of it.

Passive recruiting is something that faculty have a greater impact on than they might think. Listening to students and achieving a balance of organization and detachment seems to be one factor in student satisfaction. Faculty positivity – especially through particularly challenging semesters – is also important. If faculty are negative, it spills over into the student experience.

STUDENT OUTCOMES

Student outcomes are planned and guided by faculty. There are several shared outcomes, but in general, ideal student outcomes will differ from your institution's target outcomes. Student outcomes come down to setting expectations and goals, and building an ecosystem around what you desire to accomplish. Ideal student outcomes for SRVs include learning, skillset, mindset, resume, experience/experimentation, and monetary.

Learning

Learning outcomes must take priority over others. SRVs are for-credit courses, and without learning, they lack enough benefits to justify the time, effort, and money invested in an SRV. Generating profit is an attractive outcome for students, but the core target outcome for students when it comes to the planning stages of an SRV should always be learning.

Learning outcomes help guide high-level decisions that faculty and administrators must make when planning the course. Specific learning outcomes should be identified and applied to each potential SRV by faculty and the administration.

Skillset

Desired skillsets may influence what SRVs are created and developed on campus, what roles are established within an SRV, and other aspects of a venture. As a result of working in a student-run venture, students should develop new skills and expertise. Common skills developed include, but are not limited to:

- Leadership
- Problem-solving
- Project management
- Communication
- Sales
- Marketing

Mindset

The entrepreneurial mindset is based around continually improving skills, learning from mistakes, and taking action on ideas. Students can develop this mindset, and it will enable them to gain confidence and overcome future challenges in their own business or a corporate environment. In addition to gaining confidence and moving beyond hurdles, the entrepreneurial mindset is at the forefront of innovation. Cultivating an entrepreneurial mindset in students gets them to approach ideas and problems in a unique manner that will result in innovative outcomes.

Resume

A robust resume benefits institutions and students. The positions held by students in an SRV show employers that a student has actual business experience that they can apply to future positions. When a student can add founder or manager to their brief one-page resume, they immediately stand out among other entry level applicants.

Although many students have jobs while earning a degree, few hold management positions, and few can gain the same type of experience they receive when working in an SRV. This experience is also beneficial to draw on during interviews, because students are sure to make tough decisions, face adversity, and make mistakes that they can learn from in an SRV.

Experience/Experimentation

In an SRV, students learn about the processes and systems within a business, including finances, HR, etc. They learn how to put these together in a way that creates value for customers.

SRVs are laboratories – laboratories that come without the risks of launching a business for a student. In an SRV, students have the ability to utilize school resources and startup funds along with gaining access to fellow students of different backgrounds and abilities. This setting allows students to experiment in a safe environment to learn what works, what doesn't, how their abilities best function when working with others, and more. To do this outside of an SRV, students would need to either join an active startup as an intern, giving up time without the possibility of earning credit, or invest time and money to launch their own startup, which would also not yield college credit and would not be likely to succeed.

This entrepreneurial laboratory experience is unique and valuable. It opens the eyes of students, helping them explore whether entrepreneurship is a career path they would like to pursue while gaining new experience that can be applied to nearly any trade or position.

Legacy

An important feature of student-run ventures is the effect of legacy. Student-run venture legacy refers to the lasting achievements or impression the ownership team for a given semester or year leaves for future ownership teams and the university. Examples of legacies include: most tickets sold to productions in a semester, earning a profit to purchase new flooring for the gallery, painting or reconfiguring a space, setting up a server for hosting client projects, developing new contract templates, changing Point-of-Sale systems, being a member of the founding team of a student-run venture, etc.

Students begin to become familiar with this concept of history and legacy as part of the acquisition process. They are often impressed with what has come before, frustrated that they don't understand all of it, determined to improve upon it or add something totally new and unique. Students enrolled in student-run ventures become more aware of the concept of legacy, and it can be particularly motivating to some. Students want to be remembered for their efforts, intellect, and innovativeness.

Monetary

College courses are intended to yield college credit, not profit. In SRVs, the potential to earn both for students (credit and profit) is possible. The possibility of achieving a profit and earning a small share of that profit attracts students to SRVs. However, it should not be the driving force of their involvement due to the inconsistency and rare nature of profits in an SRV, and due to the necessity of being vested in a venture for reasons outside of profit. Still, earning money in an SRV can be positioned as an added benefit and target outcome for students.

CONCLUSION

There is no right or wrong way to operate a student-run venture. Each venture will take a different shape and form, and it's important to allow SRVs to develop naturally and grow once administration, faculty, and students are onboard. Regardless of your target outcomes as a university, allowing growth, success, and failure to happen are keys to a successful SRV ecosystem that will benefit all parties.

6. The Millikin University SRV model: frequently asked questions

Julienne Shields and Mark Tonelli

Starting a student-run venture (SRV) on your campus will be uncomfortable. You will feel out of your element at first, and you will never feel fully ready to launch, until after you do it. Student-run ventures are like startups, and you will need to take risks and overcome fears and challenges to make them work. Because Millikin has so many SRVs, we often get asked questions by entrepreneurship educators and administrators from other institutions who seek to understand our model, hopefully because they aim to mimic it at their institution. After a few years of engaging in these queries, site visits, and tours, we compiled answers to the most commonly asked questions we typically receive. If you have additional questions that are not answered here, or seek additional information on one of the answers below, we invite you to reach out and we will do our best to help further explain Millikin's unique approach to SRVs.

FREQUENTLY ASKED QUESTIONS

Why Have So Many Ventures?

At different points over the past couple of decades, we have been asked often "Why do you have so many ventures? Are the lessons learned by students repetitive?" This is a good question to ask for any fiscally responsible administrator. If you are going to invest in a venture, and make no mistake about it, there is a significant investment of time and effort made in each venture whether or not a financial investment is required, you want it to have the greatest impact possible.

Each venture is its own unique expression of students (often from multiple disciplines), faculty, industry, department resources, space resources, partners, and history. The same venture from one semester to another may have a new experience shaped from its unique actors and resources that influences or moderates the primary lessons for students. There are clear learning outcomes which are planned, but when the owner of a building with space comes in and offers a free space in a better part of town or when a critical piece of equipment is fried right before a show when the audience is already arriving, that becomes the "lesson." Important lessons often appear organically. They are not always predictable, but should be expected, and justify having multiple SRVs.

Who "Owns" Student-Run Ventures?

Mentioned throughout this book, student-run ventures are not enterprises on their own. Our ventures are backed and owned by the university. Who actually owns each venture, however, is intentionally downplayed. If students see the venture as being owned by the university, they will not develop the emotions and buy-in necessary for an authentic entrepreneurial environment and experience. Students have to be guided to believe that they are owners, and to embrace that position as an owner.

How Does Pricing of Goods and Services Get Determined?

Pricing is an interesting topic, whether the venture is a coffee shop or IT consulting firm. Students must factor in expenses and taxes when setting prices. All state and local sales taxes are reported to Millikin's business office, money is transferred internally to cover the sales taxes owed, and then Millikin pays governmental agencies appropriately.

Student-run ventures are often subsidized in some form or another by the university, the community, or specific donors. Examples might include a free space on campus in a university building, utilities, a line item for work study student employees, usage of equipment, legal advice, printing for fliers and posters, administrative support, etc. The degree to which a faculty member wishes to address these subsidies within the framing of the SRV is part of their purview.

As an example, in Blue Connection Retail Art Gallery, rent for the building is often more than 5–6 months of revenue at the gallery. Including this in the monthly Profit & Loss statement proved to be demoralizing for students in a community that consistently supports the arts by attending monthly events with free food and beverages, but is often less enthusiastic about spending hundreds or thousands of dollars on artwork. Consequently, one of the items we removed from the P&L distributed to students was the monthly rental allocation. We always told them it was there, but explained that this was something they did not have control over. The location was set, and so we removed that from their decision dashboard.

Who Pays for Startup Costs?

Startups come with expenses, both startup costs and ongoing expenses. At Millikin, the funding required to start a new SRV can come from different places, but has in large part come from our work and partnership with the Coleman Foundation. As Coleman Fellows, faculty have access to apply for project funding, including SRVs.

When starting an SRV, you need to account for startup costs and monthly expenses, which may or may not be incurred based on the type of venture. These expenses should be minimized wherever and whenever possible. SRVs at Millikin utilize university assets, from theatres to meeting rooms to transportation resources. Events hosted by an SRV may not earn much revenue initially, which requires keeping expenses to a minimum.

Can I Recreate the Millikin SRV Community at My Institution?

In the early 2000s, every Midwestern town with a few entrepreneurship advocates and innovative minds set out to create the next Silicon Valley. While there has not and likely will not be a second Silicon Valley, each town has a unique environment that can support a host of entrepreneurial endeavors.

Your university cannot become the next Harvard, nor should it try. We all have strengths, weaknesses, and resource disparities. As much as we try to overcome disparities in resources, we are constrained by them. Figure out what works for your university – what fits your environment.

Private schools, for example, have different constraints from public schools. There are different legal constraints, risk tolerance, resources, and more. To make student-run ventures work at your institution, think beyond the idea itself. An SRV must have resources, support, passionate faculty, and be a fit for your school and/or local community to achieve desired outcomes.

What Is the Student/Faculty Dynamic Like in an SRV?

The Role Clarity chapter of this book (Chapter 4) really stresses that faculty need to let go of decision-making in an SRV. Students are responsible for making decisions in a venture, and these decisions are going to be successful, or they are not going to be successful. Either way, if students are not in charge of making a decision, even a successful one, they are not learning from their decision and an opportunity to learn is lost.

While faculty can't be held responsible for making decisions in an SRV, they should provide and encourage students to seek iterative feedback. Feedback provided by faculty may not come in the form or advice, but in the form of a question. "What thought was put into this decision?" "Is everyone in agreement?" "What other solutions could be developed to address this problem?" "What type of feedback would be most helpful to receive from me and why?"

Feedback may be withheld until after a decision has been made and action has been taken. Students learn more from doing than being told what to do, which allows faculty to help students reflect on their experience and make adjustments going forward without tainting their experience.

Faculty are also responsible for facilitating discussions among student leaders and venture participants. When there is conflict between two students or groups of students, faculty should bring them together to discuss. When there are doubts about a decision, faculty can open up a class discussion to see if there are still unanswered questions, or if there is not a consensus as to what action should be taken.

Do Your SRVs Get Viewed as Competitors to Other Courses?

SRVs must be competitive, not only as profit-driven ventures, but as attractive course offerings that students want to be part of. Since an SRV requires more from a student, marketing the experience and empowering students in an SRV to market the course, both actively and passively, is crucial. There will always be easier and less risky for-credit classes, but for those who want the most out of their experience, few courses on campus can match what an SRV has to offer.

Not only do SRVs compete with other classes, they compete with everything else that is going on in a student's life. Students, especially seniors who are working on polishing their portfolios, revising their resumes, and applying for graduate schools, are busy. Acknowledging this is the first step for faculty to create the pathos and ethos needed for their students to prioritize the experience. A student once shared with Julie Shields, "Now I get it. You get what you put into it. That's what is different about Blue Connection." The student didn't understand this at first and was very frustrated. As she started leaning into the experience, she built efficacy, resilience, and leadership skills. Her peers soon followed.

How Do You Evaluate a New SRV Concept?

With 15 student-run ventures, you would think that every venture concept a faculty or student member has had resulted in a new SRV. This is not the case. SRV concepts are a dime a dozen. Each opportunity is weighed against a clear set of criteria. Institutions embracing student-run ventures need to have criteria set to evaluate new concepts.

Primarily, criteria should focus on the learning potential of the venture concept. You must answer the question, "What will students gain from this experience?" Next, the concept should be tested for viability. Can it be operated on a shoestring (or no) budget, and will the product or service be attractive to its target market? Next, answer "Will students be motivated and vested in the creation and success of this venture?" A venture concept should at least pass these basic standards to be considered for development as an SRV.

One caution when ventures are being proposed is regarding their regularity. If the intent of the venture is only to have it one semester, it becomes more of a "bake sale" than a "bakery." We are careful not to start calling everything a student-run venture unless there is a plan to make it a long-term project. We may pilot something as a topics class, but again, not label it as a student-run venture. Short-term projects/courses are welcome, but the resources available to them are different. The ability to use those courses as meeting requirements for the Entrepreneurship major, minor, and certificates is not specifically defined.

The pedagogical reasons for having student-run ventures be consistent and regular is that students need to consider decisions made in a student-run venture differently than decisions for a class project. Consequences of decisions being made by students have less tangible ramification if they don't have to live with them after the semester is over. But if a student making a decision may have to answer for it later (even if they are only enrolled at the university rather than enrolled in the course), then there is potential to be more thoughtful about the decisions being made. While consistency is not an essential characteristic, it is one that is elevated at Millikin. It also requires more forethought by the faculty and/or student proposing the venture.

Criteria, ultimately, will make evaluating concepts a quick and efficient process. These measures will be part of a living document, as changes will need to be made over time.

If I Come to Millikin Can I Tour the SRVs?

We have generated a lot of excitement around our student-run ventures. Visitors to Millikin's campus in the summer want to go see them, and they are always welcome to do so. However, the spaces that host our ventures are the least interesting thing about them. Students in action are the most compelling and interesting thing to see during a visit, but they are not on campus or working in the ventures during the summer.

The faculty are always fun to talk with, but students in an SRV are the focus and where the excitement is. Hearing theatre students talking about their unique revenue generation practices, their ticket tracking, and how they are choosing their show season based on past profitability and ROI is fascinating.

Hearing the consulting venture's practices for selecting students to be in the venture based on potential and work ethic is encouraging too. On the other hand, there are also times when a student in the coffee shop is painfully shy and not ready to confidently take a group through and articulate what they are learning. That is all part of the reality in which student-run ventures exist. It is a laboratory. Not everything is perfect.

Are Any of Your SRVs Off-Campus?

There are two off-campus ventures at Millikin. Both ventures are roughly a mile from campus, and they are excellent moderators for commitment. If a student is committed to the class, then they find a way to get there. If they are not committed, the venture might as well be in a different country. Faculty need to be mentally prepared for this reality. They can plan for 12 students in the class, but if two consistently cannot find a ride, then they really have 10, and there will be a specific dynamic for those students as they relate to their peers.

Do Your SRVs Occupy Permanent Space?

Some ventures on campus may need a dedicated space, while other ventures, as they start, are fine with just a classroom and use of common spaces. With a few exceptions, it is an advantage to at least have a dedicated space that students can "own," clean and sort, use for customer engagement, plan in, etc.

Non-dedicated spaces are particularly beneficial for developing skills that students will need as they graduate and get ready to enter co-working spaces, shared offices, etc. Learning to be productive in different locations is particularly relevant. It encourages them to not let the fact that they may not have an office shaped to their productivity or personality stand in their way. In fact, creativity may flourish in a non-traditional environment.

Is Your SRV Space Donated or Rented?

There are various ramifications tied to where the venture is housed. If the space is owned by the university, then the venture does not need to use revenues earned for the actual space. However, there is a benefit to accounting for the cost of the space per university guidelines or the market, showing the actual amount of revenue needed to offset or overcome costs of the space.

Rented spaces can work well for an SRV, but they are very expensive. Even at discounted rates, this can become a sticking point when university budgets are tight. In many cases, finding collaborative partners that value the engagement of students in their building is beneficial.

With donated spaces, there are at least three relationships to consider: the relationship between the university and donor, faculty and donor, and students and donor. If any of these relationships becomes stressed, the other two will be impacted, and challenges may arise.

How Do You Maintain Consistency Semester After Semester? Do You Ever Pause SRV Activity?

Student-run ventures are courses, and courses require consistency. This consistency can be every semester, every other semester, or at other regularly scheduled intervals. An intermittent venture is fine as long as there is a brand, an effort to build and recruit for the venture, and a meaningful reason for the discipline's curriculum.

Pauses are welcome if needed. A good example of that is with the Big Blue Personal Training venture. The entire curriculum for personal training went through an overhaul, and students who would be trainers in the venture would no longer be eligible as juniors, but would need to wait until later. This meant that there would not be adequate numbers of trainers for a long period of time. Given all the other conditions within the department, it was advisable to pause the venture itself, and include entrepreneurship in students' curriculum as infusions into other courses.

What's the Lifecycle of an SRV?

Not all food products can gain the designation of being organic, but a larger portion can be labeled as natural. SRVs are not organic – they are forced. However, as mentioned above, they must fit your school environment. Our ventures are formed as naturally as possible, and they die as naturally as possible as well. There is no set lifespan for an SRV. Some ventures last a semester while others survive through multiple decades.

Student-run ventures that continue to survive year after year often have gone through creative destruction and rebirth along the way. All businesses go through change and many have to reinvent themselves. What worked in the 1990s is not likely to work in 2020 and beyond. Launching a venture that can work within an institution's environment and landscape is one challenge to overcome; adapting to changes to continue is another that will be up to faculty and student leadership groups to figure out.

Each venture has their own path and story. Not all student-run ventures that began still exist, and others developed and proposed through a business modeling plan were never launched. What causes a venture to come into being or continue to exist is not simply the local marketplace, though. The main questions are "Is there a curricular need?" and "Does this further the long-term goals of preparing the students for their careers post-graduation?"

There is a commitment to take each prospect of a student-run venture with earnest enthusiasm. Faculty, students, and community partners with a commitment to extend the mission of entrepreneurship make the case for an SRV and how it will fit into curriculum, be covered by faculty load, and avert budget constraints. And given all these factors, at the time of this writing, Millikin still has 15 SRVs. What works best for your institution will develop over time through learning and collaboration.

How Is an SRV Different from Other Campus Programs and Activities?

Many activities around a college campus are extremely close to a student-run venture. Here at Millikin, there is a student-led investment portfolio, a non-profit endeavor to provide weekend meal backpacks to at-risk students in the community, a theatre project that reduces recidivism in the local prison through Shakespearean productions, and more. Some of these activities are only missing the formal designation of "student-run venture" at Millikin because their faculty may not have been Coleman entrepreneurship fellows, or because there are so many student-run ventures on campus it may be considered too common to be distinctive. But these also are all essential entrepreneurial endeavors, and many campuses have similar kinds of activities being taught as courses within their respective curricula that would be considered under the definition of student-run ventures.

How Are Faculty Compensated for Overseeing an SRV?

Student-run ventures tend to be relatively low-enrollment courses that take an especially high level of faculty time to run effectively. Faculty do get to count the SRVs as in-load courses they are teaching, but they are not provided any additional stipend or release time for overseeing them. The faculty who lead our SRVs do so because they are passionate about the mission of the venture and because they see a lot of pedagogical value created for the students involved. Yes, they would each tell you that leading an SRV is more work than prepping and teaching a new course, but they would also tell you that they love working with their SRVs and they chose to take on this effort (leading an SRV has not been forced on anyone; forcing someone to lead one seems like a strategy for failure – you need faculty who are willing and passionate).

Certainly, each university can come up with a model that works for their institution and faculty compensation structure. There is no right or wrong answer to compensation and each university needs to implement a structure that works within the nuances of their structure. We fully support compensating faculty appropriately for their time, but are also cautious about balancing that relative to compensating at a level that the additional money becomes more of a motivator than passion for the venture and student opportunity.

How Are SRVs at Millikin Different from SRVs at Other Universities?

All SRVs are going to look and feel a bit different based on the students involved, the faculty leader, and the university and business environments in which they operate. Millikin has done a good job of maintaining a common definition and philosophy about SRVs across the whole campus, but each school at Millikin does approach these in a way consistent with that school's staffing and student base. We see similar nuances when we look at SRVs at other universities – they all vary to some extent. What sets Millikin apart is, perhaps, the success we have had in scaling these to disciplines all across campus, growing a movement on campus for these to thrive, and successfully securing partnerships with the business community to operate some of them off campus (whereas many other universities focus primarily on on-campus SRVs, though there are exceptions).

What Are the Main Points of the Value Proposition You Would Stress if Putting Together a Proposal for an SRV at Another University? What's Going to Get Administrators and Community Members Interested and Engaged?

It is important to stress the curricular alignment and how the SRV is going to further the entrepreneurial endeavors within the department or industry in which the venture is situated. If it is a music SRV, how is it positioned to help students see themselves as music industry entrepreneurs post-graduation? How the venture will prepare them for the promise of that major or degree is a significant consideration.

Space utilization and location are also essential. The location will dictate so many aspects of the advantages and challenges of the SRV. On campus ventures are easier for students, but limit the kinds of interactions with primarily university-affiliated customers/clients. Off campus ventures require a higher degree of commitment from faculty and students, but the richness of the customer interaction is palpable.

Have You Ever Had an SRV Fail So Badly It Had Significant Negative Consequences? Are there Major Risk Factors to Manage?

No, but there is a story that highlights the unique situation of SRVs being affiliated with a university and all the politics therein:

There was a situation once where an SRV instructor was approached by an artist who was the relative of an administrator. This artist asked for a better percentage of the proceeds when their art sold than was typically covered in the contract for non-student artists. The instructor facilitated a discussion among students about the request, and the students determined it was not appropriate to bend the rules for the artist just because of the relation. Now, it's not clear how much of the process of letting the students debate and make the decision was adequately conveyed to the relative. But the result was that it caused grief for the instructor as well as the artist. The administrator expressed some concerns with how the relative was treated. As an artist/entrepreneur, one could argue that the lesson learned there was that you don't always get what you ask for.

Is something like this a major risk factor? It could be depending on the goals of the faculty member, particularly if tenure is a goal and objective. But, again, understanding the culture of your institution is important when setting the expectations. By and large, most failures truly are learning opportunities.

Is Social-Loafing a Major Challenge within the SRV Courses?

Social-loafing is certainly a challenge for which to plan, and it is a good focal point in the development of faculty. There are some contributing factors for faculty to consider. Why are students taking the class? Is it a requirement for their major or program of study? Did the student self-select into a functional role within the SRV, or did the instructor put them into a role because of their major or some kind of preconception about the student? Were they recruited by a friend to be a part of the course?

If a student is interested or passionate about doing something specific within the experience, that plays a role. Some students don't know what they want to do, so extra attention is needed by faculty to draw out possible areas of contribution. Other students are the dynamic leaders who may struggle to delegate to others, so they wear themselves out while contributing to the malaise of their peers.

If they are taking it as a requirement for their degree, then there are those who do not see entrepreneurship as an important set of skills for their own future careers. These are the toughest ones, in our experience. The ambiguity of the experience along with a lack of personal entrepreneurial passion is a toxic recipe. Each faculty has to address this with their own skills and talents. We have seen faculty turn some students around by giving that student the most important task for the SRV for the semester. It is an experiment.

Some strategies for combating this have been utilizing Agile or Scrum methodologies with daily or stand-up reports, reflection sessions where students are encouraged to share face-to-face what their peers are doing well and what they could improve on. "Carrot" peer pressure tactics often seem to work better than others. For some students, discussing legacy of their semester or their tenure with the venture is a motivating factor. Identifying strategies for combating social-loafing is complex, but the tools available for faculty in SRVs to combat the issue are certainly more varied than in traditional classroom experiences.

7. Reacting to crisis: how student-run ventures pivoted following the 2020 COVID-19 pandemic

Mark Tonelli

On March 11, 2020 the World Health Organization declared the COVID-19 (aka coronavirus) a global pandemic, representing the falling of the first major domino in a long line that quickly created challenges, both long- and short-term, for the majority of people around the globe. Most universities abruptly shifted to exclusively online education, emptying dorms, canceling events, and closing campus common spaces. Similarly, everything from small businesses to beaches to restaurants closed, remote work became the new normal for most non-essential employees, and almost all travel halted as many cities around the world began issuing safer-at-home orders, encouraging people to stay home. For student-run ventures this meant a lot of change, both from the educational perspective and from the day-to-day operations perspective. Given this book was being compiled just as all of this was happening, we felt it prudent to memorialize the impact of the pandemic on SRVs. Thus, this chapter shares, in their own words, SRV faculty perspectives on the pandemic and its impact on the student-run venture courses they oversee, and offers practical steps to addressing a crisis such as this in the classroom.

FACULTY PERSPECTIVES

RJ Podeschi

I was particularly impressed with the way students in MUPC handled the global pandemic. Students recognized that it would be more difficult to obtain new clients given the economic environment and limitations to meet in-person with others. However, they knew the technology existed for them to continue work on existing clients virtually, and redirect their attention to the future of the firm rather than the present. Consultants continued to attend at almost 100% participation in our weekly Scrum meetings via Zoom and used Slack as the main method of communication throughout the week. Some consult-

53

ants continued to be focused on recruiting new consultants for next year by visiting other professors' classes via Zoom to get the word out and scheduling interviews with potential candidates. One group of consultants focused on rebuilding the MUPC website (www.millikinpc.com) and the marketing team built brand awareness through Google AdWords campaigns, blogs promoting existing client work and how work continued in light of COVID-19, and spearheaded a social media initiative to get other students to register for student-run ventures. Another consultant built scripts to automatically populate student time sheets and generate analytics based on their work log data. Work certainly slowed down, but consultants were resilient in taking initiative and finding ways to move the venture forward.

I can't say it was all sunshine and rainbows. A few students had barriers that limited their ability to contribute as much as they wanted. Whether it was an additional job or being a caregiver, students were definitely placed out of their normal university life. When asked, students consistently said that meeting virtually was difficult. Students couldn't rely on body language as much, and valuable (although distracting) side conversations couldn't take place. Furthermore, students had a hard time really discussing and working through problems in a Zoom call. They said they felt like they were just reporting out to me, and not each other. They had a hard time adjusting to the ground rules of an interactive online meeting. There are some pieces there that likely need to be strengthened in the future if more meetings take place via Zoom.

That said, I feel they found comfort in MUPC that it was a departure from a normal class – that it gave them additional energy because they were passionate about its purpose, and they weren't satisfying typical course requirements, but their own goals in addition to MUPC's.

Stephen Frech

When the COVID-19 pandemic hit, we were forced like everyone else to move our course online. Because the course is dependent on equipment and hands-on learning, we had to find a way to move forward with as many print projects as we could manage and with student learning. We decided to shelve all print projects but a book cover we were sub-contracted to provide for a new book publishing venture on campus. This job had commitments to fellow students in another course and to an author under contract.

Design work continued remotely, looking at type samples, proofs, and color schemes. We discussed our options and made decisions together. Then I became the sole set of hands on the equipment in the shop. It was not ideal, but the learning shifted from mechanical craft (developing proficiency with the equipment) to design. In this way, the class pivoted in virtual delivery by de-emphasized craft and emphasizing design.

Letterpress printing provides great opportunities to practice design. It's a discipline that works with fixities: physical objects, lead or wood type in set point count, and images that cannot be altered. So designers in letterpress must solve visual problems in three dimensions—they do not have the tools of computers to alter the scale of objects, to photoshop images, or bend/reshape text. We have physical objects and we must design with those objects as they are.

These seeming limitations result in wonderfully imaginative solutions: color as a compositional element, layering of images and text or "bleeding" them off the page. Blue Satellite Press attracts graphic design students from the Art Department every year, and the course always challenges them to rethink the habits they've developed as designers trained almost exclusively on computers, with all the up-to-date digital tricks.

To complement the learning on this cover job, students found letterpress designers online whose work they liked and wrote three-page papers analyzing the aesthetic and the decisions those designers made to achieve the look of the work they produced.

Sara Theis

This semester was difficult for the Pipe Dreams Studio Theatre (PDST) team. They were one week from opening their spring rep when we moved to the online format. All of their money was spent in terms of salaries and materials. They had sold very few tickets so far to the shows but that is not unusual for them. The duration of the semester shifted to mitigating expenses (e.g., asking for refunds for things like performance rights, returning purchases where they could) and increasing engagement with audiences. The panic that everyone felt in terms of "what do we do now?" was no different for the members of PDST. They froze. It took some time and once they were ready to get going the university was beginning its big fundraising campaign and they had to pause. Ultimately, the group was able to cut enough expenses and raise enough money to break even. The class took a pass on salaries so that they could pay the artists they had contracted to work. They came super close to breaking even. Moving into Fall, we worked over the summer to determine what that looks like in terms of creating work and connecting with audiences. They have chosen a season that resonates with their classmates and everyone is excited about. We do not yet know what reality will hold in terms of live performance.

Mark Tonelli

It is important in a crisis to take into account the level of disruption that people are experiencing. During quarantine, academics encountered frequent advice to be sensitive to the extra burdens their students might be carrying, including moving back home unexpectedly, having to take care of younger siblings, poor internet connection, loss of employment, and depression. As a result, how we evaluate students may need to shift. A pass/fail option is one possibility, and some institutions did adopt this policy. Other students may require more specialized consideration. For example, I had one student during quarantine who had been missing class regularly, something this student had not done while we were meeting in person. This student lost the campus jobs that were the student's primary source of income. Eventually I received an email, which said the following:

> This whole situation with online classes and the pandemic in general are affecting me more than I imagined it would. The assignments are starting to become over-whelming for me. I struggle to have mental focus or clarity when trying to complete some of my work. I wanted to apologize because I know I am just incapable of being the student that I was last month and prior.

This letter put a name, a face, a real person to the sometimes abstract concept that "some" students were facing overwhelming challenges in their lives. It caused me to realize that some of my own students were probably facing greater challenges than I was observing in the short space of two 50-minute classes per week, even if they said they were doing fine when I asked.

An online course is not necessarily intrinsically easier than a face-to-face course. What some teachers may be concerned about, however, is the loss of rigor that suddenly transitioning online could present, that students are not receiving the full experience that the teacher perceives they need. We are, after all, preparing students for professional life, and we do not want to skimp on vital areas. In a time of crisis, however, some reasonable concessions may need to be made. Insisting that every last assignment be done with pre-crisis capability may not be the best approach. At the same time, it may also not be necessary to scale back on rigor. There are some intermediate options, like extending the deadlines on assignments or revising the requirements for certain assignments to conform to whatever conditions a crisis may present, as Arts Café did with its transition to virtual shows.

Naturally, the quality of students' work may diminish in a crisis, but eval-uating them on pre-crisis criteria may just not be fair. Take into consideration what the student is capable of at that moment and evaluate accordingly. Many posts from colleagues in the COVID-19 support group I was a part of stressed the need to balance flexibility and compassion with academic rigor, and if nec-essary, err on the side of compassion. Hardline approaches in a time of crisis may only further aggravate a student's circumstances. Likely, any concessions on the side of compassion will go much farther in the long run in helping a student. It is certainly better to be remembered as the professor who worked with a student to help them in a time of crisis rather than as the insensitive professor who callously demanded that all work be done with exacting detail. A little compassion can go a long way.

STEPS TO ADDRESSING A CRISIS – AN ARTS CAFÉ EXAMPLE

SRVs are inherently innovative. A theme that runs through the case studies in this book is how students or faculty members frequently fail in their efforts within the context of an SRV. That failure is often desirable, because it teaches the student or faculty member to internalize rejection and use it to improve for the future.

Acknowledge. The first step is to acknowledge that a crisis is a difficult situation, and accept it. Another thread that surfaced in blogs and online support groups during the pandemic was the pressure many faculty members felt to be productive, perhaps even over-compensating by being over-productive. This could lead to feelings of guilt or inadequacy. It is important to allow yourself as the faculty member or administrator to feel badly about a crisis. Do not attempt to mask or smother how you are feeling by artificially busying yourself with extra activities to counterbalance for a perceived lack of productivity. Just process your feelings in a natural way. Advise students to do the same. Take a class period or two to let students talk about how they are feeling. The solidarity of hearing that other people are feeling similarly can be cathartic. Getting it off their chests can enable students to move forward.

Make a plan. Do not get stuck in this mode and wallow in self-pity. After allowing people to air their feelings, it is time to move on. The next step is to make a plan. Fortunately, an SRV has a built-in team, and the faculty member alone does not have to be responsible for solutions. This is truly where the *power* of an SRV can be accessed. One example of how this process worked is with Arts Café's "pivot" to online operations.

Rely on the collective. After an extended two-week spring break, Arts Café's classes had transitioned to an online format via video conference. The first class was exclusively a check-in to see how students were doing. Some were visibly shaken and unsure of the future. Others enjoyed the solitude and time for reflection. Suffice it to say, things were not normal, and the students were struggling. Upon reflection, this class period seemed important, as it allowed the students to process what they were feeling and move forward. At the next class period, Arts Café shifted gears. Arts Café is a live performance venue. Much of its aesthetic revolves around the in-person aspects of energy, décor, vibe, and interaction with the audience, intangible pieces that are nearly impossible to replicate virtually. The thought of losing these pieces of Arts Café's core identity could easily have defeated the students. Instead, relying on each other for support, and in typical Arts Café fashion, the students bounced ideas off each other about what to do next. This "spitballing" phase has always been a staple of Arts Café's creative process, the laboratory where ideas are born, and the consistent practice students had with it served them well during the crisis. Ultimately, the students decided to reframe their vision and view the pandemic as an opportunity to explore a new medium – streaming online performances. This was not a perfect process. There were certainly bumps along the way. Some students missed classes or got behind in their tasks, partially due to the disruption they were experiencing in their lives. In this less than ideal situation, however, the students showed great fortitude and resilience, and the transition was ultimately quite seamless. This was in part due to Arts Café's artistic director, an incredibly optimistic and positive person, who kept people motivated and excited to re-imagine the venture. This further reinforced to me the need to have a strong leader at the helm. In turn, Arts Café's already-planned in-person shows were canceled and a new slate of online shows were planned, in what were called "Virtual Shows." Some of these shows were simply a digital version of what would have been live shows; others were wholly new creations.

For instance, a pop singer-songwriter student from Millikin was Arts Café's first online show. This artist had an online following and was savvy with respect to marketing, and many of her fans (who were not familiar with Arts Café previously) attended the show. She took the time to make the physical space visually appealing, with good lighting and an artistic backdrop. In addition to strong original material, she had a polished stage presence and an engaging on-screen personality. She kept things moving in between songs with witty banter. Overall, the students judged Arts Café's first online show as successful, which validated their choice to move events online and encouraged them to keep going.

Assess and revise. Arts Café's second online show featured a rapper, also a Millikin student, whose original material was very strong. His friendly personality in between songs was engaging though his banter was not nearly as polished as the singer-songwriter's. The physical aspects of the presentation were generally not well-planned. He broadcast from his living room, with dim lighting. His assistant's head poked in and out of the foreground, which was a distraction. There were some technical problems with cueing up his backing tracks. The students quickly realized how spoiled they were with their first online artist, who was intentional about the overall production of her show, an element that Arts Café usually controls. They assessed what went well and what they could do better and began to revise their procedure for creating an online show. For example, noting that they would have to find ways to control the visual presentation moving forward, Arts Café inserted language in their artist contract that provided for audio and video checks to ensure a higher quality presentation.

Seek new opportunities. Beyond merely moving what would have been an in-person show to a virtual show, Arts Café realized that the advent of shows could present opportunities that were infeasible in-person. Arts Café could now contract artists who may have been inaccessible previously due to distance or cost or other prohibitive factors. As an example, Arts Café's third show, "Martial Arts Café: Self Defense For Everyone" featured a national champion martial artist, Cathy Ciciola, who lives in New Jersey. The cost of bringing Cathy to Illinois from New Jersey could have easily wiped out Arts Café's budget, but with an online platform, she was now a viable option. Cathy and I were friends in undergraduate school. I had followed her rise as a martial artist over the years, and I suggested her to the students. From there, the students took over and handled every aspect of producing her show online. It was a completely new experience for the students in Arts Café to work with an artist outside the Millikin community, where most artists have tended to come from. The students were able to see a broader view, something that had always been envisioned as part of the course but never got off the ground. The pandemic now provided this opportunity. What had started as a problem became a solution.

What you keep. By semester's end, the majority of Arts Café's shows – four of six – had been streamed live online. The students found value in this new approach, which allowed them to explore new areas they could not have reasonably explored before. Therefore, as they move forward in future semesters that meet face-to-face, they may retain some elements of their online experience. They may create a hybrid series, in which some events are in-person, and others are online. Alternately, they may decide to revert to all in-person events, but if inclement weather (primarily snow in Illinois) threatens to cancel an event, they could move it online. Their experience with a crisis provided them with a new skillset. It broadened their palette of creative choices. Ultimately, it made them more flexible and adaptable to change.

Every crisis is different. It is important to recognize that different crises will present different challenges and, therefore, different solutions. The COVID-19 crisis is isolating people and forcing them to find solutions that tend to be virtual. Virtual solutions, however, are only one type of solution. There surely are other types of solutions in the current crisis, and some people are employing them.

In future crises, isolation may not be the primary limiting factor. For example, as this book was nearing its very last stages, the tragic death of George Floyd and the subsequent outcry presented a second type of crisis, an ethical and not physical one. Despite months of warnings that large gatherings would create a "super spreading" event, which would lead to exponentially more COVID-19 infections and deaths, large groups of people began to gather in protest of Floyd's death in a call for radical systemic change in combating racism. It appeared that the needs of the newer crisis superseded the needs of the older one, and gathering now *was* the thing to do. Proponents for social justice felt they could not achieve unity and solidarity virtually, and that gathering was necessary. It remains to be seen whether such gathering will have led to a rise in COVID-19 infections, and it should go without saying that in any type of response to a crisis within the context of an SRV, we must place the safety and health of our students first. Nonetheless, the nested crises the world experienced underscores just how diverse responses can be to a crisis and how, in turn, we must allow our students to develop unique solutions to unique crises. For example, it is conceivable that if we had not been in quarantine during the death of George Floyd and it had happened during the semester, Arts Café could have produced a live event to raise awareness in support of fighting racism.

CONCLUSION

Arguably, the COVID-19 pandemic is the largest mass intervention to date on entrepreneurship education (Liguori & Winkler, 2020). It may be years before economies recover and universities re-establish a new normal for how they operate. Student-run ventures, like all ventures, must learn to operate in a new environment, which while not ideal for many reasons, does create an opportunity for student-run venture student leadership to develop resiliency and practice agility in responding to ever-evolving market conditions, two

Figure 7.1   Arts Café virtual show screen capture

essential characteristics of successful entrepreneurs. Excitingly, our students are open to learning, so if we teach them to remain agile and give them the tools needed to pivot, they can accomplish amazing things. Figure 7.1 shows one such example, an Arts Café virtual show conducted during the 2020 COVID-19 pandemic.

REFERENCE

Liguori, E., & Winkler, C. (2020). From offline to online: Challenges and opportunities for entrepreneurship education following the COVID-19 pandemic. *Entrepreneurship Education and Pedagogy*, 3(4), 346–351.

PART II

Student-run venture case summaries

8. Pipe Dreams Studio Theatre

Sara Theis

INTRODUCTION

Artists often hear that their wishes to become professional artists, actors, theatre owners, or musicians are just "pipe dreams." We work to make these dreams come true at Pipe Dreams Studio Theatre (PDST), a theatrical industry learning laboratory that was created through a collaboration between Millikin University's School of Theatre and Dance and Center for Entrepreneurship. PDST is a student-run venture that offers an environment for artists to learn, play, experiment, and explore by presenting theatrical experiences intended to challenge audiences to question their perceptions of art and its connection to the human experience.

The Fall of 2011 marked my first semester of teaching full-time. As an instructor of Stage Management and Theatre Administration, PDST was a very intriguing part of my course load. From the first class, I could tell that the students were in it to *show* me, the new kid on the block, how they could successfully run a theatre. This was an exciting year for the PDST as it marked the first semester they would charge students for tickets. As you can imagine, there was resistance to this change.

PDST, as a student-run venture, began in 2010. Through PDST, students interested in the arts are tasked with running the theatre as a business. As you can imagine, students are more interested in creative work than in preparing spreadsheets. At first, it was difficult to convince students that writing down expenses, collecting income, onboarding employees, organizing work, and setting goals were important activities. As theatre students, these students had only been exposed to the process of making, and not the business work that goes on behind the scenes to make that product possible and profitable.

Productions are not cheap. To raise money for PDST, students launched a successful Kickstarter crowdfunding campaign that raised $500. To increase awareness of the theatre and to promote events, students worked to find marketing opportunities. They were able to get the PDST coverage in *Thrive Magazine*, a publication that promoted local arts programming through a community calendar and articles on local arts happenings.

Before becoming a student-run venture, Pipe Dreams was more of a lab than a business. It was a space in which students would show off their original work at no charge for other students, and the department was required to attend performances. Now in charging for tickets and seeking to bring in revenue in order to produce licensed work, students faced an uphill battle. The students running the venture were organized and determined, and had a lot on their plate with planning the Fall semester season, which included two original works, two licensed produced works, and gay cabaret.

They were also delving into the world of contributed income. After having success with their Kickstarter campaign, students were planning a live fundraiser, which they planned to promote at Arts in Central Park, an arts festival with vendors from around the region. They secured an exhibit table, created flyers to hand out, and planned a schedule for student workers to promote the fundraiser at the Arts in Central Park event. Promoting the fundraiser meant that one company member would stand behind a plastic 6-foot table with a piece of poster board taped to it that read "Pipe Dreams Studio Theatre" in sharpie. The table stood out, but not in a good way. Arts in Central Park was a heavily attended, professional arts festival with art and artists on display. Booths had attractive signage, cash registers, intricate designs, and more.

I went to the festival to support two of our student-run ventures who were exhibiting at the event. When I approached the PDST table, the company member was optimistic about their success so far. "I handed out a bunch of flyers and spoke to a few people!"

The following Monday, I followed up with the class to see how they were feeling about their investment in the Arts in Central Park event. "How did everything go this weekend at Arts in Central Park?"

I heard a mix of positive reviews: "Good ... Really good ... Great!"

"Awesome, that's wonderful," I said. "How are you feeling about the fundraiser?"

I heard a similar mix of positive responses: "Good ... Really good ... Great."

"Oh, that's wonderful," I said. "How many people do you think are coming?"

I could visibly see the confidence and enthusiasm in the room begin to dwindle. "We don't know," they said. Wanting to build them back up while helping them move forward, I offered a suggestion. "That (how many people are coming) might be good information to have. Is there a way to set up an RSVP system?"

I was stunned by what happened next. Although my memory may be a bit flawed when it comes to recalling every detail, they responded with a gesture. The class collectively put their index fingers to their lips, shook their heads at me gently, and said, "Shhh. Shhh. Shhh. Shhh. Shhh. Sara, we are Pipe Dreams. Perhaps, you have heard of us? We've been in *Thrive Magazine*. They will come. There is no need to worry about such details."

Instead of doubting *them*, I began to question myself. Who was I to teach this class? I had been involved in fundraisers to benefit theatre companies where there was some form of entertainment. There were tables of people who had spent money just to be there. There were silent auctions and live auctions and multiple ways to donate. But, I had never once been in charge of making sure everything went according to plan. I was always in charge of the production part of the evening, and that was it. I had not set the goals. I had not created the invite list. I had not reached out to people individually to make sure they were coming. I honestly did not know how any of that happened. At this point, I was making assumptions. After all, this was a student-run venture. Who was I to tell them that they were not taking a successful approach?

The class continued with planning the entertainment for the evening. I watched as a million thoughts and questions ran through my mind. One of them slipped out, and I asked, "Who have you spoken to about coming? Do you have any confirmed attendees?" My questions were not well received, and I was told that they had already reached out to the VPAA (Vice President for Academic Affairs), who would be in attendance. They continued to work out the logistics of who was performing when, how they were going to arrive at the venue, and what food would be served.

I listened further, and more questions began to slip out, "Have you thought about how people will donate? It might be fun to think about how we might approach that?" Again, I was met with disapproving looks. The class, collectively, in a disapproving tone, said, "Sara, this isn't that kind of party where you *ask* people for money. That's crass. This is more of 'an envelopes on the table' kind of event. There will be a silent auction but that's just for ambiance. People will just give us money. Did you not hear us before? We are Pipe Dreams." After being squarely put in my place, planning continued leading up to the event, which was just three weeks away.

The night of the event, I walked into the Arts Council hoping to be proven wrong. I saw a cash bar, hors d'oeuvre, silent auction, a piano being played sweetly in the gallery, and the talent all set to perform the evening's entertainment. It was a beautiful venue, exciting lineup, and a very well put together fundraiser that was attended by two faculty members from my department, the dean, and the VPAA. A total of four people outside of the Pipe Dreams team were in attendance, boosted to five with my appearance.

The logistics were flawless; food was delicious; entertainment was engaging. There were envelopes on the tables, a silent auction prepared, and a cash bar ready to go. The VPAA decided to turn the event into an open bar using his credit card, and then left. The silent auction sold one or two items, but it was never collected because students did not ask for the money after the conclusion of the auction.

The following Monday, it was time to talk about the "fundraiser." I knew that they would be disappointed at the attendance, but grateful about the lessons they had learned. I asked, "How are we feeling about it?" The response was not exactly what I was expecting. "Oh my gosh! It was amazing! The food was great. The entertainment was entertaining. The bar was open. What more could you ask for?"

"Excellent! What were your financial goals?" I asked.

"Food! Entertainment! Open bar!" they responded.

"Yes. All great. What were your attendance goals?" I asked. "Food! Entertainment! Open Bar! Did you see our pretty envelopes? They were on the tables," they said collectively. It became obvious that they were indeed disappointed, but did not want to relive their experience. I needed to address it head-on. "It is okay to have things not go the way you want them to go," I said. "We need to discuss it and figure out how to make it better next time. Let's talk about it so we can solve it." It was then that the conversation opened up. We discussed hard things like setting goals and evaluating performance. We further defined our collective vision for the future and figured out how we are going to get there. We made concrete observations like the fact that we needed a confirmed guest list to shoot for in the future to avoid having only a handful of faculty attend.

My role as the teacher became clear at this point. This was their company, their ideas, and their vision. They were in charge of everything and could do it. I was their subconscious. My role was to help them recognize their flaws in thinking, challenge their assumptions, and give them the tools they need to solve the problems they have. When I worry about something, they dig deeper into it. When I ask how they know something, they make a case. When I offer tools to help them think through an issue, they use it to create a solution. It's a good relationship, and it was built on top of a tough situation that I had to allow happen in order to get to a good place.

DISCUSSION

The class itself is limited to 16 students and is a variable 1–3 credit hours. Students typically take it for the maximum their schedule allows. It is made clear from the beginning there is no difference in workload whether you take the course for 1 credit or 3. This course has a reputation for requiring a lot of work, and it is true. It is also an elective. Students take it because they are invested in the success of the company. Many see it as their artistic home. This is the place they get to be decision-makers. They decide what to do and how to do it. They get the excitement that comes with executing all parts of the process of the company. They own both the successes and failures – it all belongs to the students running the company.

The company's structure, from an organizational standpoint, has changed multiple times. In the beginning, people interested in being part of the executive team (Artistic Director, Managing Director, Production Manager, Marketing Director, and Director of Public Relations) interviewed for those positions the semester prior and held the position for one semester. During the first planning process, students immediately understood the need for more institutional knowledge. Coming into an executive team position requires knowledge to maintain continuity for the organization itself. Additionally, they acknowledged a need for a change in the structure of the leadership team to better serve the organization, so they changed several key roles. Students also decided to institute a policy that in order to serve as a member of the executive team, one needed to have been enrolled in the class for one semester prior to applying. Students in the class who were not members of the executive team chose their job title and the tasks they would complete.

Budgeting and tracking expenses were not a thing they wanted to engage in, so it was left untouched as something they just didn't get to until semester's end. There was not a long-term plan for the season and the artists all did the work for the resume credit.

Over time, the "one semester prior" policy was replaced with a policy that serving on the executive team would now require a three-semester commitment. Roles and how those were chosen, also began to change. Students realized that others in the class who chose titles were choosing them based on what they wanted to do and not what the company needed. PDST had more Event Planners and Archivists than one company could possibly use. Those titles really meant that students wanted to throw parties and take pictures of the work of others. PDST eliminated job titles for non-executive team members and moved toward project-based work. New roles on the executive team were added only when needs were identified and a student with drive and vision to solve that need emerged.

Currently, PDST has the following positions on the "executive team," Artistic Director, Managing Director, Production Manager, Marketing Director, Director of Development, Director of New Works, and Director of Education. Executive team means that students have applied for and been offered a top-tier leadership position within the organization. Competition for these roles is tough and students take it very seriously. Students who have been offered an executive team position make a three-semester commitment to the class and are responsible for programming in their area.

The company's view of budgeting and tracking changed as they saw a need for tools. The need came when musicians said they needed to be paid for their work, and the company saw that as a reasonable request they had to plan for. "Musicians" eventually became "all artists." "All artists" eventually became "everyone who works on shows." "Everyone who works on shows" eventually became "all those who add value to the company."

Students are paid a stipend for their work in PDST. Students who are "hired" by the company receive payment when their work is completed. Students who are enrolled in the class receive a stipend at the end of the year and that amount varies depending on the budget surplus the company achieves. Students have set two strategic goals regarding artist payment and budgeting. First, they recognized the need to get better at budgeting after reviewing how far off their budgets were from actual numbers. They are now actively trying to create budgets within 10% of actual numbers.

The second initiative focuses on increasing artist salaries to half of market value. PDST recognizes the value that artists bring to their company and wants to compensate them accordingly. They spent time determining what market value is in the region and made some significant changes to their business model in order to accommodate the increase. On an ongoing basis, they are looking for ways to improve efficiency to reduce costs, and increase income to continue increasing artist salaries.

Interim Semester

Students spend their first semester planning the season, and all the parts that have to work together. Students call this the "interim" semester. The next two semesters are focused on executing the plan. Planning starts with the basics – articulated mission, vision, and values of the company. These were formed early in the company's history and remain intact for all teams. From there, the executive team dives into strategic planning to see where the company is headed. Then, we discuss what each team wants to accomplish in the upcoming year. These goals vary quite a bit from team to team, and have included "increasing attendance," "creating more opportunities for students," "improving experiences for artists," "improving experiences for customers," and "engaging more of the surrounding community." We then create programming, calendars, and budgets that align with our goals for the upcoming season.

The structure of the mainstage season varies from year to year, and the number of productions can range from 3 to 4. There is typically a mix of musicals and plays. Students understand that musicals tend to sell better but are more expensive to produce, so they have to budget accordingly.

Everyone has an opinion when it comes to agreeing on the best route to take. The goal is to choose programming that aligns our value proposition and brand with work that the students are excited about producing from an artistic perspective. PDST has worked hard to differentiate themselves from other offerings in the area, both on and off campus in order to create a unique value proposition. The hope is that this will engage a larger audience and create a balanced budget so that work can continue for another year.

Balancing the budget is a difficult task for a theatre company. Earned income does not cover expenses. The Director of Development puts together a plan to make up the gap through contributed income. This plan typically consists of grants, a fundraising event, and some form of individual giving campaign. Contributed income makes up about 20% of the overall budget. Planning in this area comes with strict guidelines, and we differentiate between goals and budget numbers. They can set whatever goals they want when trying something new. However, income can only be included in the budget if they have received it before and have a reasonable expectation that they will receive it again at the same level.

Students set goals for engagement numbers and create programs to increase those numbers. One of those programs is the New Works program, an all-night play festival in which teams work to create a play overnight, and a New Works festival, which presents newly developed plays in front of an audience. New this year, we've added an education program where students work in schools and with community groups to allow elementary school students to develop and perform their own plays.

The planning semester ends with dreaming big about how this season will be the best ever for PDST.

Fall Semester

In student-run ventures, students quickly realize that dreams may not reflect reality. The Fall semester typically sees the big dreams from the interim semester dashed as the real world and real people make their way into the equation. From the students' perspective, everything goes wrong and nothing happens in the way it was supposed to happen. They learn to adapt and deal with challenges.

In reality, nothing has gone wrong. People are people. Artists are artists. Customers are customers, or they are not. We learn hard lessons about collaborating, managing, and resources, and how all the planning in the world cannot accurately predict what will happen when it is time to execute. They learn that we have to keep a close eye on how we are doing on all sides in order to reach our targets, and they learn that no individual department exists in a vacuum.

Spring Semester

In the Spring semester, the venture runs smoothly. Students attain goals they set for themselves and finish the year with a small surplus. They also end the semester with more wisdom and confidence. They come to believe they have something to offer and see the need to offer it to the incoming executive team. They spend lots of time training and warning against making the same mistakes, and they offer opinions on what could be done differently to make it better.

ASSESSMENT

Like everything else in the class, assessment has evolved in order to make stronger connections for students between their classwork and final grades. The current breakdown is 60% Sprint work, 10% Big Business Project, 15% Self and Peer Evaluations, 5% Engage with the Industry Project, and 10% Do or Die. Specifics on each of these are discussed in detail below.

Sprint Work

The class uses agile methodology as a system of management in the classroom. Agile grew out of the IT world and provides a platform that allows a team to respond to changing circumstances and alter their work accordingly. It gives ownership to students who may not know what to do when first entering the class. The system encourages open communication and asking questions. It also helps prioritize what needs to be done so completed tasks are those that will be most impactful. Overall tracking of work is also simplified.

Each project in agile is called a sprint. Prior to the start of the semester, we decide which projects will be completed, when that work will be done, who will lead the team, and how many team members each project requires. The goal is for each student to work on three teams, and we shape projects and teams until we hit that number. Typically, there is a requirement that everyone has to do one sprint dealing with producing the show, one related to meeting income and attendance goals, and a smaller project stemming from the many other ideas students develop. It took a couple of semesters to figure it all out, and it has been a game changer. Table 8.1 shows a sample schedule. See also Figure 8.1.

Students keep track of tasks they complete, and at the end of the sprint, submit a "board report" (see Table 8.2) listing those tasks, identifying the

Table 8.1   *Sample schedule*

Week of:				
8/26				
9/2	**Produce Shows**	**Plan Marketing**		
9/9	**Pat-rice**	**Sophie**	**Dennis Ed.**	
9/16	Taylor, Audrey,	Kenzi	**Maya**	
9/23	Shawn, Maya,		Taylor	
9/30	Mel, Steven,			
10/7	Mason, Emily			
10/14	Melanie, Triston			**Recruiting**
10/21	Carrie	**Income/Attendance**	**Community Ed.**	**Melanie**
10/28	**Maintain Shows**	**Sophie, Kenzi**	**Maya**	Emily
11/4	**Pat-rice**	Audrey, Carrie,	Taylor	**Tech Cab**
11/11	Emily, Melanie	Mason, Emily, Mel,		**Kenzi,** Triston
11/18	Steven	Melanie, Triston,		Steven, Sophie
11/25		Shawn		**All Night Play**
12/2				**Mel,** Carrie, Pat-rice, Mason
12/9				

goals or "deliverables" of the sprint, and offering a short assessment of how their work contributed to accomplishing the goal. In addition, they submit a post-mortem reflection based heavily on Heidi Neck's work in *Teaching Entrepreneurship: A Practice-Based Approach.* Their teammates evaluate their work and contribution on a Google form. Packets are then evaluated using the rubric below. The question of impact helps the individual student and team leader realize the importance of prioritization and accomplishing high-value tasks.

Big Business Project

The company works on one large overarching project over the course of the semester. This may be strategic planning, feasibility testing, stakeholder needs assessments, or annual reports. We have done strategic planning four times over the past eight years. Typically, plans are written to be completed in five or more years. Often, they are in place for as long as institutional knowledge of the previous process lasts, and then it is time to do it again. Feasibility testing occurs when there is an opportunity the company wants to dig into. Annual reports are conducted every spring as a way for the outgoing team to articulate what they have accomplished. These projects lead to documents future teams

Source: © 2020, Herald & Review.

Figure 8.1   Rehearsing for Carrie the Musical

can look to for direction when they are creating their seasons to help them identify strategies to reach those goals. This project is typically worth 10% of the final grade.

Self and Peer Evaluation

Fifteen percent of the grade is comprised of a final self-evaluation and an average of their peers' evaluations. The self-evaluation is a 3–5 page paper in which students reflect on what happened over the course of the semester, what ideas and practices they want to build on, and what changes can be made in order to help things function more smoothly in the future. There are typically some "aha!" moments for students in this exercise once they are able to look back at all of the events of the semester and put their thoughts down on paper.

Engage with the Industry Project

The Engage with the Industry project is worth 5% of their final grade, and is a small project or paper helping them engage with the larger arts community. This has typically been a review of another company's work or an interview

Table 8.2   *Sample board report*

Deliverable	Impact	Scope of work	Completion	Obstacles	Post Mort	Board report	Peer evaluation
Deliverable is absent/not defined and not produced (0)	Contribution will have no impact on the deliverable (0)	Scope of Student's role in the deliverable is undefined or absent (0)	Student did not do the work (0)	Obstacles were not dealt with (0)	Post mort is absent (0)	Student did not submit board report and did not attend meeting (0)	/25
Deliverable is absent/not defined or not produced (9)	Contribution will have minimal impact on the deliverable (9)	Scope of Student's role in the deliverable is minimal (9)	Student did minimal work (9)	Obstacles were dealt with minimally (9)	Post mort is under-developed (9)	Student did 1 of 3, report, format, meeting (9)	
Deliverable is somewhat defined and produced (18)	Contribution may impact the deliverable (18)	Scope of student's role in the deliverable is marginal (18)	Student sometimes did the work (18)	Obstacles were dealt with marginally (18)	Post mort is marginally developed or does not meet the due date or format (18)	Student did 2 of 3, report, format, meeting (18)	

with someone who is working professionally in a role similar to theirs in the company.

Do or Die

"Do or Die" makes up the final 10% of the class grade and is based on whether they make their income and attendance goals for the semester. They set their own goals for these during the planning semester, and they can be as high or low as they like as long as their budgets balance.

Thinking about the business side of the organization is not something students are very excited to engage in. Do or Die was added a few semesters ago to give students an opportunity to work on their art. This addition to the syllabus has helped boost attention in this area. It took one semester of not making "Do or Die" for students to get serious and realistic about their income and attendance goals. This has also helped with the budgeting process because they have to balance it with more realistic income numbers.

OUTCOMES

Time and time again, students tell me they feel more professionally prepared as a result of taking the PDST student-run venture class. They leave this experience with many takeaways, including:

- Knowing they have made an actual impact on an arts organization.
- The ability to articulate their impact on resumes and in interviews.
- Knowing they can overcome challenges and work toward productive solutions.
- The understanding that nothing in the market is absolute and they need to find ways to respond to changing circumstances.
- The knowledge that planning is not a substitute for sound judgment in the moment, but helps an organization make critical decisions.

Here is feedback from several former PDST executive team members:

> *My expectations for Pipe Dreams were to be given a list of already chosen productions by my professor, told how much money we had to make on each production, and instructed on how to do it. The minute I stepped into that room, the line between professor and student was blurred. It was a group of people, committed to run a business together and make decisions to make it flourish. The event that really surprised me was having to present a budget in front of a real board. I remember thinking, "This isn't a class at all. This is a real business, with real stakes. Holy crap, this is my career in action." The challenge of being a managing director for an arts based company was finding the balance between doing meaningful art and doing art that would fuel the business and bring in funding. Even so, it's something*

that I am grateful to have learned in a college environment rather than on the first day of work in the "real world" ... I will say it again, for me it was never a class and never felt like it. It was my business, my company at the time. And I'm glad so many after me can say the same.

Pipe Dreams Studio Theatre was by far the most challenging, thought provoking and rewarding experiences during my college years and has been invaluable in my following career. As a student-run venture, it was more than just reading about the field – it was about actually getting my feet wet and doing the work. While I do believe traditional classroom work and case studies are an important foundation for learning, this hands-on experience allowed me to get a true taste of what my field would actually be like to work in. This allowed me to realize for myself what my strengths were in additional to determining what skills I needed to continue to work on.

At this moment in time, each piece of how this company works belongs to the company member who made it the way that it is. Nick Throop created the organizational structure of the organization as it stands. Mikey Mulhearn set our artistic direction and aesthetic. Blanca Hernandez began the process of forward thinking in terms of the budget. Tyler Hixson introduced us into the world of grants and streamlined our calendar. Ashlee Kline got us thinking about ways to engage audiences beyond ticket sales. Taylor Stuenkel clarified our budget system and introduced us to prediction. Ike Brown took prediction one step further and began applying it to ticket buyers and show selection. The list goes on. They all grow. They all learn. They all have an impact. They all leave their mark.

CONCLUSION

Student-run ventures still need help. There have been "interventions," and yes, I mean the kind where an addict's family and friends sit them down, tell them how much they love them, and encourage them to make big changes in their lives. When asked to address a problem, change the way they are thinking about something, or think about an inequity in a way that they feel is not immediately achievable, students, typically a couple of executive team members at a time, will schedule time to talk. When they arrive, they sit down, lean forward in their chairs with their forearms on their thighs, and ask questions like, "Are you sure this is the choice you want to make? Do you understand the implications of it? Do you know what the words you are saying mean?" and, "How do you think this makes us feel?" They say they are worried there is no understanding of the implications of what is being asked, or that people will quit, or how this will mean the end of Pipe Dreams because they cannot possibly do it.

Interventions happen because things get stagnant and we stop challenging ourselves. We lose the vision of where we are heading and need to find it again. Or sometimes, there is another way of doing something that we need to explore. These students are capable of more than they imagine for themselves. Our role as educators is to open doors so they can clearly see the path in front of them. We are not doing it for them; we are challenging them to understand that for every problem there is a solution, and they are capable of finding it.

Ideas for Teachers

Spend time dreaming with students. Discuss what a student-run venture they could successfully create and run on your campus would look like. Then, create goals for the organization. We create stronger ownership when we are clear about what we are working towards and students feel like they have had a voice in creating those goals. They want to do great things. Let them dream it, define it, and do it. Challenge students to think beyond the status quo. As undergraduates, they have not yet been exposed to all the ways a problem can be solved. Give them the tools and options for what success might look like and the ownership to implement solutions. Finally, budgets and financial planning are vital, and not as complicated as we might think. We can accomplish our mission and achieve our vision if we have the resources to do it. Money is one of those resources. Without it, neither the mission nor vision of the venture happens because our doors are closed. Get comfortable with the idea that a budget is a plan, not a bank account, and plans are made to change. The bottom line is what matters. If a group of our young artists can come to realize this fact, then your students surely will as well.

9. Art Circus

Dave Burdick

Art Circus was a not-for-profit student-run venture dedicated to recognizing and showcasing diverse talents through events that provide audiences with an impactful experience in an aesthetic atmosphere. The idea for Art Circus sprouted from my participation in the 2013 Global Consortium of Entrepreneurship Centers (GCEC) conference in Kansas City.

After listening to Michael Morris' keynote address on how entrepreneurship is used to solve complicated real-world problems in underdeveloped world economies and inner cities, I had a vision. I had a vision of student artists taking control of their own artistry, bringing their talent to the marketplace in unexpected venues, and teaming up with other artists to create unexpected experiences for audiences. I saw "rings" of artists with a ringmaster directing the audience's attention from one performance to the next. I saw Art Circus.

There were many well trained and diverse artists at Millikin – both in and outside of the School of Music – who rarely, if ever, got to take their art outside of traditional performance practices or venues. I saw an opportunity to reframe what artistic performances could look like, but curricular solutions were not well-suited to tackle this "problem." The idea for Art Circus was to develop performance concepts with artists and create a unique context for events.

Using a pilot course number from the Registrar's office for Art Circus, it was listed in the online course listing for the Spring 2014 semester. I used email and word of mouth to promote enrollment and ended up with a class of around ten students. The Center for Entrepreneurship made us a weekly evening class, meeting in a media enriched conference room in the business incubator on the edge of campus. The conference room helped set a tone of professionalism right out of the gate, which the students seemed to thrive on.

Students were put in charge of developing the culture, organizational structure, and leadership structure of Art Circus. The culture of Art Circus developed as an open environment for ideas and collaboration. As the "coach," I remained patient and made sure all voices were heard. Art Circus wasn't going to rock the world in one semester; we wanted to build something durable.

Exercises in creating an organizational structure proved premature and largely pointless. It was clear that we weren't going to create realistic job titles and responsibilities until we started staging events. Students who stayed in Art Circus for multiple semesters gained hard-won experience, and were able to usher in newcomers effectively. I've heard more than one colleague address how, without experienced leaders, their venture kept reinventing itself without gaining traction. Starting over each semester is not ideal. Student-run ventures should move towards maturity while remaining receptive to the ideas of new students, which eventually led to the development of the organizational structure, along with other aspects of Art Circus.

Rapid prototyping is a common action taken by entrepreneurs. The idea is to put your product or service into the marketplace in its early rough or unfinished form. The purpose is to observe your customers and solicit feedback from them. As I said above, Art Circus needed to stage an event before we were entirely sure what one of our events would look like. In our second semester (Fall 2014), we settled on an event called Sunset at the Sunken Garden. In front of the library on the Millikin University campus was an enchanting but seldom used outdoor space one story below ground level. Hardly anyone on campus knew about, let alone used, the sunken garden.

We stuck to a modest plan for the event so we could collect and process the data. We employed a few singer-songwriters, a hula hoop dancer, and a DJ. To help attract an audience, we included food and a modest $1.00 ticket price. Using a portion of Coleman Foundation grant money, we purchased hotdogs, buns, chips, and some charcoal to use on the grill located in the sunken garden. Millikin has a partnership with Pepsi, which enabled us to obtain three ice chests full of Pepsi products for free.

Luck was with us – we had a glorious autumn evening and a modest audience of around 40 people. This crowd allowed us to cover food costs, but we fell short of paying performers.

We learned many valuable things from our prototype event. The audience liked the idea of a variety of artistic disciplines being represented at a single event, although they were not fans of the DJ. Once the DJ began performing, attendees quickly left. Attendees noted that they loved the ambience of the space and the food and beverages. We also tested out the idea of the Art Circus Ringmaster – the character who ushered the audience's attention from act to act. After numerous post-event discussions, students decided that Art Circus would do a sunken garden v.2 event in the spring.

Event analysis led us to the following improvements:

* We would diversify the types of performances by commissioning interdisciplinary talent to create something unique.
    * Building on the overwhelming success of our hula hoop dancer from the first event, we commissioned a four-piece percussion ensemble to compose and perform two pieces for her to dance to.
    * We envisioned a piece called Shakespeare Then and Now wherein a classically trained actor would recite a Shakespeare monologue accompanied by period-correct lute music, then tear off his costume revealing contemporary hip hop attire and rap the same monologue to a custom track created by a beat producer.
* Understanding the intense amount of oversight it would take to manage the two collaborative performances, we turned to three existing acts to fill out the show:
    * An all-female acapella group.
    * An all-male acapella group.
        * Making effective use of the space, both acapella groups were placed along the walls of the sunken garden to create a 360° listening experience with the audience surrounded by performers.
    * A popular and accomplished acoustic pop group capable of extending the event by performing as people entered the event and in between the other artists' performances.
* To make the event more "circus-like," we:
    * Brought in food vendors and artists to do face painting and hair braiding.
    * Continued to develop the Ringmaster character by letting him create his own costume and write his own script.

Immediately after the upcoming Spring semester was finished, the library would undergo demolition prior to the new university center being built onto the front end of the building. Included in the demolition plan was the sunken garden, which would cease to exist. That inspired the name of the v.2 event: Farewell to the Sunken Garden.

With the many improvements made to the event by students, Farewell to the Sunken Garden was wildly successful. Pre-event tickets, which were $3, sold quickly, and sales at the gate nearly doubled as we welcomed almost a hundred students to the event. Attendees polled after the event said they had never experienced anything quite like it, that they loved the unexpected combination of performers, and they loved that performers were in different positions relative to the audience. This event cemented the role of the Ringmaster, who became a beloved figure and the signature of future Art Circus events.

Though the Millikin Center for Entrepreneurship described the student-run venture as a lab experience as opposed to a lecture, I routinely taught entrepreneurial principles. In the interest of developing competencies and sharpened analytical thinking, I focused on teaching principles in the first semester.

One thing I tried as Art Circus matured was doing entrepreneurial case studies. I was referred to a book by Katz and Green (2009) titled *Entrepreneurial Small Business*. Each case study came with a set of discussion questions, which students loved. In particular, they liked being able to focus in on key "pivot" moments in cases; points where the entrepreneur at the center of the story had to make decisions they didn't expect to make and confront unexpected outcomes as potential growth opportunities. These studies hammered home the fact that entrepreneurs need to stay nimble and be adaptable. Those were takeaways that had a direct impact on how students thought about Art Circus.

The Spring 2016 semester included an important success *and* a failure – both of which are equally important to the long-term success of a student-run venture. I had an experienced group of students that semester, and we decided to divide them into two project groups. Each group was responsible for hosting their own event.

The first group took on a project called Night of the Diva. The concept put singers of classical art songs and opera on stage at a nightclub on the edge of campus known for rock bands and open mic nights. The Diva team, under the leadership of one of the best leaders we ever had in Art Circus, booked the club date immediately, and then worked to create the best event possible from that starting point.

To make the event feel exclusive to artists, the team held auditions. A poster campaign and some personal selling brought plenty of artists to auditions. Once the roster of artists was agreed upon, the team helped artists select material to perform, worked with them to develop a stage look and manner, and educated them on how to use an area mic on the stage. They hired the best student accompanist in school for two rehearsals and the show. From there, the rest of the planning consisted of simple tasks. They used a trusted graphic artist to design posters and tickets, which were sold in advance at a discount and full-price at the door.

This group of students also figured out how to co-promote through social media. The team linked up with the venue's social media accounts, which helped promote the event to members outside of the Millikin student body. The team also leveraged the social media accounts of each artist. As expected, performers brought many of their own followers to the show, and there were also many audience members from around town.

During the event, the audience quickly became absorbed by an event they would never have otherwise seen. The audience responded quickly, and the performers fed off of this energy, delivering dramatic and heartfelt performances. Night of the Diva made enough money to pay everyone and put some cash into our reserves. It also made a lasting impression on the planning team, audience, and performers.

While the Diva team was working on their event, the second team went to work on an event they called the Cell Phone Film Festival. This team struggled to gain traction. They spent valuable time brainstorming on the same issues over and over again instead of agreeing to basic aspects of the event and moving forward. The name of the event changed multiple times, the guidelines and categories changed again and again, and other details, including the target market for the event, shifted constantly. Each time one aspect of the event was changed, they would revisit previous decisions as well. Spending time on the same issues prevented the team from being able to promote the event to filmmakers and audience members.

The team finally secured an interesting venue, but it was off campus and too far to walk for students. The team now had to approach campus safety and security to offer van service for students to and from the venue.

I prodded the Film Festival team to make their weekly goals clear to themselves and to the class, and to try harder to move more deliberately and decisively. As you might imagine, the whole project eventually fell apart, and the event never happened. Although the Film Festival team had some wonderful ideas and a lot of potential, they fell short on feasibility issues, lacked a clear vision, and failed on all matters of organization.

At the end of the semester, I brought in a guest panel for the two teams to present to. The Film Festival team did an excellent job identifying the shortcomings of their process and offered a much more realistic plan that they would tackle were they to try it again. One realization that came out in discussion was that they had failed to apply the lessons of the two Art Circus Sunken Garden events: how to keep a first-time event feasible so that you can grow into a more ambitious version the next time around. The Cell Phone Film Festival was definitely a prototype event for Art Circus, and a more modest frame around the project would have increased the chances that it would have happened, and with some success.

Sadly, Art Circus came to an end after five semesters. I had a great class that last semester, but it was loaded with graduating seniors. Two of the newcomers had both changed their majors and decided to transfer to schools closer to home. I was left with one student. At the same time, Mark Tonelli had talked to me a few times about his idea for Arts Café. Rather than restart Art Circus from the ground up and create venture redundancy within our program, I decided to move on and create a new student-run venture. The new venture is called

MIST (Music Industry Studies Tour) and was conceived as an entrepreneurial solution to address the lack of an ensemble performance program for students who want to perform popular music. That, however, is a story for another time.

OUTCOMES

Most of the outcomes that I was looking for would be classified as competencies; that place where skill meets the entrepreneurial mindset. Entrepreneurial competencies are highly valued by Millikin's Center for Entrepreneurship and appear regularly in their curriculum. These are the particular competencies that I targeted as an indication of student learning in Art Circus:

- Opportunity recognition
- Problem-solving
- Leveraging resources
- Communicating a vision
- Adaptation/learning from failure
- Value creation
- Innovation

I also looked to see if students were gaining a sense of risk and reward, meaning they accepted risk as the "nature of the beast" but knew the difference between risk and recklessness. Finally, I looked for some passion for our projects in students and to see if leadership was developing. Leadership did emerge organically with certain students, but I struggled to engage more reserved students to display leadership traits.

Profitability is important in every business, but in a student-run venture, learning comes first. I placed some importance on profitability as an outcome, but I was mostly looking for us to operate "in the black." Some of my colleagues have student ventures that are surprisingly profitable. Profitable student-run ventures tend to offer services that are in demand in the marketplace to a greater extent than what Art Circus was offering. Put another way: Art Circus revenue was dependent upon an audience rather than a client. In its most mature stretch, Art Circus succeeded in spending money to make money. The fact that it wasn't a lot of money didn't hamper student learning.

Table 9.1 shows the financials associated with Farewell to the Sunken Garden in the Fall 2015 semester. Keep in mind that we were a non-profit organization and only kept enough money to contribute to our small operating fund.

Our financials were never impressive, but as a learning experience, we created and executed an impactful event with a lot of moving parts, and we still came out in the black. If Art Circus had a longer run as a venture, a similar

Table 9.1   *Farewell to the Sunken Garden financials*

Ticket Sales Revenue: (98 customers X $3.00/ticket)	**$294**
Expenses:	
Graphic design of posters and tickets:	$40
Printing of posters and tickets:	$15
Payouts to venders**:	
Face Painter:	$27
Hair Braiding:	$16
Family Recipe Chili:	$35
Baked Goods:	$20
Payouts to artists:	
Acoustic Pop Group:	$0*
Female Acapella Vocal Group:	$25
Male Acapella Vocal Group:	$25
Shakespeare Then and Now:	
Actor/Rapper:	$15
Lute Accompanist:	$0*
Track Producer:	$15
Dance Suite:	
Hula Hoop Dancer:	$15
Percussion Group:	$0*
Art Circus profit after expenses and payouts:	**$46**

Notes:
* Services donated.
** One dollar from each ticket sold went to a coupon that audience members could redeem for a vendor service/product.

event marketed to the Decatur community may have drawn in more revenue, and possibly enough to have paid our artists closer to what they were worth.

Another important outcome was for Art Circus to have a strong sense of identity. I was extremely happy with how Art Circus envisioned, created, and ultimately *acted* upon our mission. The Art Circus mission statement, mentioned at the start of this chapter, was beautiful and well crafted, and I'm proud to say that I had absolutely zero to do with it – that was entirely student work. It did, however, take three semesters to clearly understand our mission and be able to craft that statement.

ASSESSMENT

Given that Art Circus was a laboratory experience and students were taking it for a single credit, I assessed student learning through their personal reflections and team presentations. Those activities can both demonstrate a synthesis of ideas and actions. There were some traditional homework assignments, including readings/discussion questions, and other written assignments, but I viewed those more as preparation-for-class assignments that created a baseline of consistent grades (attendance, preparation, participation).

At the end of the semester, when it was time to take stock of our intentions versus our results, I had student teams prepare a detailed report of their projects – from inception through process to result – and deliver this report to a panel of guest entrepreneurs. The members of the panel asked questions and delivered feedback to engage the presenters in discussion at the end of the presentation. It was always a great moment of learning in large part due to students embracing their failures *and* building off of their successes. Peer teams (it was common for me to have two separate projects going at one time in Art Circus) were present for each other's presentation and free to engage in the discussion at the end of each. I stayed out of the proceedings myself while taking notes for my final evaluations.

I evaluated for:

- Clarity of the presentation
  - Expressing the vision
  - A clear and organized storyline
  - Effective use of media technology to support the presentation
- Team members display growth in entrepreneurial competencies
  - Opportunity awareness
  - Problem-solving
  - Resource leveraging
  - Adaptation
- Project management
  - Leadership
  - Team structure that affected how the project moved forward on multiple fronts
  - Nature of relations with outside parties contracted for services
- Some amount of quantifiable data in the telling of the story *(such as)*
  - Number of consumers of the product/service; level of customer satisfaction
  - Costs
  - Income
  - Analysis of digital media marketing strategy
- Ability to understand and respond to questions from the stakeholders

- Honest reflection on what they would have done differently (and will do differently next time around – typically a discussion point entered into with the guest panel)

I led periodic discussions with simple questions:

- Why did you do what you did?
- How did you do it?
- What did you think would happen?
- What actually happened?
- What did you learn and how can you adapt?

These are all simple questions that, if legitimately reflected upon, yield great moments of learning. In Art Circus I was able to offer reflection guidelines as part of the framework for the end-of-semester presentations. I also used reflection questions as preparation for post-event analysis and discussion. The question that unfailingly demonstrated that my students were learning was, "What will you do differently next time?"

Art Circus Student Testimonial

Art Circus is the real deal.

We would dedicate a healthy portion of each class to brainstorming our next entrepreneurial venture, whether it be as a whole or in smaller groups. Class discussion encompassed a wide variety of topics, and included ideation sessions, research presentations, planning strategies, prioritizing projects, assigning tasks, mapping, and executing our goals.

My favorite part about Art Circus was having the chance to learn the basics of event production. The experience aligned directly with my double major in Music Business and Commercial Music when we produced "Night of the Diva," at Donnie's Homespun Pizza.

After graduation, I went on to work for an event production company in Chicago for 2 years. Many of my roles at this job were similar to those I had as a student in Art Circus; event planning, researching venues, summarizing projections, managing contacts and budgets, attending meetings, organizing and sharing creative ideas while achieving reasonable deadlines.

I have since started my own LLC as an event DJ, and work as an Executive Assistant to Entrepreneur, IP Attorney, and CEO of the Everyday Inventor, Keith Cyzen.

Hannah Poorman
DJ / Vocalist / Creative Producer
www.bonafidevox.com

CONCLUSION

When empowered to make decisions over their learning activities, students rose to the point of ownership, they appreciated and valued that it was their ideas being put to the test, and they enjoyed being allowed to fail at something without having to worry about earning a low grade.

Sometimes the issues you encounter in class will leave you feeling like you're on thin ice in terms of your ability to teach through the issue. Perhaps you find yourself needing more knowledge or a finer awareness of entrepreneurial skills. First, let me say that when that happened to me early in the Art Circus journey, my students were more than happy to see me as a fellow learner rather than a professor with all the answers. You do not need to have all the answers; those come along the way. Second, I have yet to be refused by a colleague to whom I turned for assistance.

We had received grant money and used it to acquire certain equipment, had hired a graphic designer to create promotional materials, had invested in food supplies to sell refreshments for a small profit, had invited a variety of niche vendors to ply their trade at the event and paid them, while disbursing payment to the participating performers. In short, we had money coming and going in all directions. The beauty of that moment lay in the fact that we all realized right there why accounting was a valuable skill! I immediately contacted a colleague of mine from the accounting department and she spent two class periods demonstrating the fundamental elements of accounting, and then she helped us set up our first legitimate ledger.

Another lesson I learned is that games and exercises can assist students in discovering a solution, as opposed to reading or being told about a solution. So if the group is suffering from communication breakdown, there are communication games and exercises you can engage them with, which will show them the essential points of clear communication.

Once in Art Circus, students were having a challenging time explaining their ideas for an event in concise terms. I found an exercise that suggested students draw their idea on a single piece of notebook paper or napkin, and show it to ten people outside of class to see who can accurately describe the idea. It turned out that by taking words out of the equation, students found a more visceral expression of their idea, one that communicated a feeling.

I want to leave you with a final message – don't wait around until you feel like you've been expertly trained to teach entrepreneurship. The important lessons are learned along the way. Jump in the same way a first-time entrepreneur jumps in to start a venture and learn on the fly. Some twenty some years ago, at the start of my second personal venture (Thirdstone Productions), I hung a postcard on the wall with a caption that read: Sometimes you have to make the leap and build your wings on the way down. Take that leap, then empower your students to build the wings.

REFERENCE

Katz, J. A., & Green, R. P. (2009). *Entrepreneurial small business* (Vol. 2). New York: McGraw-Hill/Irwin.

10. Blue Satellite Press

Stephen Frech

Blue Satellite Press is a student-run literary letterpress publishing company. It was founded in 2008, making it one of the longest, continuous-operating student-run ventures in Millikin's healthy ecosystem of student-run ventures.

Blue Satellite began as a publisher exclusively of letterpress poetry broadsides: a single sheet of paper, much like a poster, featuring a poem. The appeal of these broadsides resides in the high production value of traditional letterpress print method. It's reasonable to assume a market for prints bridging the divide between literary off-set publishing and fine arts prints. Having our hands in two seemingly different worlds of publishing didn't expand our market or audience, it simply made us strange to both simultaneously. Over time, we expanded our catalogue to include other items: coasters, bookmarks, poetry pamphlets, and a line of fun greetings cards called *Cheeky Greetings*.

Student-run ventures and entrepreneurial course components are rare in English departments and the humanities at large. There may be a myriad of explanations, but the predominant one is simply habit. Entrepreneurship historically has not been part of the traditional literature and humanities curriculum. In truth, humanities disciplines have prided themselves on their remove from marketplace considerations. "Art for art's sake" has been a persistent and persuasive mantra. The merits or implications of "art for art's sake" is a debate for a different occasion.

This chapter presents Blue Satellite Press as an example of a successful student-run venture in an English department, one that provides practical, vocational experience for students going into design and publishing jobs and historical, contextual knowledge for students who pursue literary ambitions.

And it provides a real-time model for engaging a community, entering a professional conversation, and developing credentials. The model established from the very beginning was a venture that could pay for itself, even if you couldn't or didn't want to make it your vocation.

My students, like students of all disciplines upon graduation, enter a challenging job market that is changing faster than ever. My students, as English/ Creative Writing majors, are entering a job market less willing to recognize the critical thinking skills so many humanities disciplines rightfully claim. Employers and students alike are seeking instead surer, short-term skills that look more like vocational training of a white-collar variety.

I can help by giving humanities students professional skills, a curriculum that blends learning and practice, and a model for self-sustaining business ownership. My students can remain active as creative artists, engage the literary community around them, and cultivate a community that is truly their own.

DISCUSSION

In the course that operates Blue Satellite Press, students perform all aspects of a literary publisher. They serve as editors, identifying living American poets whose work they like, soliciting unpublished poems from them, and choosing which of those submitted poems we want to publish. They design and layout the publications. And they learn the craft of letterpress printing: hand-setting text in lead or wood type, carving plates for imagery, and operating the presses.

The course is high on the craft of letterpress printing. Students rarely know exactly what letterpress printing is, let alone have any experience doing it. So we devote the lion's share of our time to production:

- learning about the equipment (knowledge is the best safety)
- learning the process
- learning the history and cultural value

All of these complement each other in important ways, and the problem-solving they learn to master in three dimensions models the more abstract skills of assembling ideas and text.

Course and Curriculum

Blue Satellite Press is a variable credit English course – students can take it for 1–3 credits. Most opted for 3 credits, but some students enjoy the 1- or 2-credit options if their schedules are already full, and they're eager to take the class. The course is an important contributor to our department publishing courses, our professional writing concentration in our writing major, and our publishing and editing minor. Students can take the course as many times as their schedules allow, growing in expertise and the commensurate roles that run the venture. Students who take the course multiple times graduate with a full set of skills that lead to jobs in publishing and editing.

Enrollment is a persuasive argument in course proposals: will students take the course? Will they return? And can the course succeed in producing experiences and artifacts that appeal to students and contribute to their learning? So piloting the course becomes a critical test case in departments that might be skeptical about such a course. A first semester should be carefully prepared for students to do a full-scale launch or start-up and to produce the first quality product. Each subsequent semester should bring some project to completion. A course that produces only projects that require multiple semesters to complete (letterpress printing is labor intensive, and publishing books takes time) runs the risk of losing student momentum and interest. Smaller projects in Blue Satellite have allowed students to see projects from conception to completion in the same semester, while they contribute to longer projects that span several semesters.

Again, some colleagues steeped in the traditional literature curriculum may be resistant to what looks like vocational training. A publishing course, however, provides an important lesson in historical context for other literature courses. Benjamin Franklin and Mark Twain both cut their teeth as writers in print shops, setting text in movable lead type. And students gain an important understanding of the cultural value of text once they learn the labor necessary for printing books. Lord Byron, soon after the instant fame resulting from *Childe Harold's Pilgrimage*, sold the entire first run of 10,000 copies of *The Corsair*. What commitment must a publisher make printing 10,000 copies of a book by a 26-year-old poet? What labor must he or she invest in printing 10,000 copies? Students come to understand the magnitude of these numbers when they have to hand-set a poem in lead type.

Self-Sustaining

Students in the arts and in much of the humanities don't have the advantage of business creation initiatives as a part of the traditional curriculum, and they come to embody the attitudes of the culture around them as it relates to business and the arts: chiefly that the two cannot coexist. Or, if they do, someone or something has been compromised. This is a dangerous and disabling attitude, but it's all too prevalent in the arts and humanities.

To be fair, letterpress printing went largely out of commercial use and transitioned into a boutique industry for good reason: there are cheaper, faster printing methods available today.

By self-sustaining I'm referring to a business model that allows students to start their own small literary presses, collectives, or residencies without jeopardizing their livelihood. Running an arts organization (literary press, small theatre troupe, etc.) may not provide one's livelihood, but it shouldn't jeopardize it.

It's imperative to be honest with my students about what they are learning in a letterpress class and its commercial value.

1. It's highly unlikely they will pay their rent (let alone feed themselves, pay for insurance, etc.) as a letterpress printer.
2. They can learn a craft that still translates well to design, publishing, and printing industries.
3. They can learn to engage a literary community, shape their own small literary circle by publishing books, journals, broadsides, or zines.

This last point cannot be overstated. Many writers fresh out of undergrad, even after MFA programs, watch their classmates scatter into a variety of gainful employment. They too will need to pay the rent. How then to maintain a vital connection to literature? How will they find their own tribe when the posse of school and workshop has split up? How do they keep themselves engaged while they cultivate their own craft?

Publishing a journal (or books, chapbooks, etc.) must truly be a self-sustaining venture. Students must be able to launch such a venture with minimal initial outlay, and they must be able to maintain it outside their already tenuous household budget.

So how do you make such a venture sustain itself? It takes the course to adequately demonstrate, but here are the basic start-up nuts and bolts.

Expenses and Income

A small venture like Blue Satellite benefits by keeping things simple. Your non-business students will appreciate the accessibility of clear, simple break-downs. Expenses versus income. For Blue Satellite expenses include equipment (presses, drying racks, portfolios), consumables (ink, solvents, paper), time, labor, postage, and marketing (flyers, copies, etc.). Income results from sales, commissions, or contracted projects.

The equipment is housed in my letterpress studio, so those come at no cost to Blue Satellite as part of the course. Figure 10.1 shows a student and me in the studio. If students were to replicate what we do together on their own, they would likely have to rent time in a studio at about $25 per hour. We can estimate that expense to see how close we are to breaking even in a model that would require renting the equipment. And the time and labor, I tell my students, will go unpaid. So too likely will be the hours they devote to developing their skills as poets or writers. So if we set aside those two expense categories, we are left with consumables (inks, solvents, paper) and the recurring expenses (e.g., postage). Each broadside costs $50 in paper, $45 in shipping, $15 in ink, and $5 in solvents, for a total of $115.

Figure 10.1   Working in the letterpress studio

We have recently printed broadsides in runs of 80 prints. Students new to the discussion will want to multiply the number of broadsides (80) by the retail price of each ($15). "Wonderful," they say. "We will make $1,200." But you can't sustain a business on impossible ideals. We give 5 free copies to the poet. Now we have only 75 prints. And we sell extra copies to the poet at a 50% discount. So a self-sustaining venture asks a different question instead: how many broadsides do we have to sell at retail to cover our material expenses? Eight broadsides at $15 each totals $120.00.

The prospect of running such an enterprise without it costing any money, without it draining one's household budget looks much more attainable. Sell 8 of the 75 copies and the publisher has covered their material expenses.

Literature in all formats (books, chapbooks, prints) all sell better at events with the author present. So, the poets can sell their broadsides much more easily than we can. They buy them at 50% discount, take them to readings, and sell them at full retail. So, a different way of determining sustainability is to ask "how many broadsides do we sell to the poet at 50% to cover our material expenses?" Sixteen broadsides at $7.50 each totals $120. Even if the poet only buys 10 extra copies totaling $75, we can cover our material expenses by selling only 3 broadsides at full retail. Any of these sales models is not only realistic, but it's so attainable that students begin to realize they could launch their own ventures without losing money. And they begin to imagine ventures and initiatives that could benefit and delight them.

Over three years Blue Satellite has earned $484 and spent $367. These numbers don't establish false hopes about students earning a livelihood printing letterpress poetry broadsides, but they do inspire the realistic hope that students can launch a venture of meaning, creative inspiration, and professional value without draining their household budget. Ultimately, whatever the detailed mechanics, art and writing students benefit from a discussion of realistic, self-sustaining venture strategies.

Price Point as a Signal of Value

Blue Satellite Press started selling broadsides for $8. I had assumed that carefully considered poetry and a quality print would appeal to buyers. But readers of poetry often questioned a print for a single poem that cost as much as a whole book of poetry. And our prints are modest enough (both in size and cost) that art buyers didn't see a place for them in their collections. The quality of the prints quickly improved, and we continue to add and improve print techniques with each project. As the catalogue grew, the number and variety of poets began to appeal to a wider audience.

As Blue Satellite developed and won a small but devoted following, we re-examined the price as part of wondering about the early lackluster sales. $8 didn't really tell people the true value of the broadside – what it was, how it was made: a signed, limited-edition print. It simply looked like an overpriced piece of paper (albeit artisanal quality). Raising the price to $15 immediately told buyers that there was something special, rarefied about them. People stopped at the display to take a closer look – why is this print $15?

The price point also allowed us to comfortably offer buyers a variety of deals such as 10% off with cash or if they bought more than one print. People like to save money. Two people often try to pay separately, each one buying one broadside. We can charge them together and offer them the discount of purchasing more than one print and save them both money – buyers are delighted with the deal, and we can operate in the easiest currency of cash.

The proof of price signaling value revealed itself in an immediate jump in sales that then became the new status quo for Blue Satellite Press. Price point tells buyers important information about what they are buying and its value relative to the market and other items they buy.

Zen of Being in Control vs. Letting Go

Learning is key for students, and it is equally important for faculty too. As the academy generally moves away from faculty-centered pedagogy, other varieties of pedagogy have had to take its place. Student-run ventures, by their very nature, have been learning laboratories that seek to develop authority among the students, not keep it centered on the professor. What is the nature of student-run ventures?

As a veteran teacher of creative writing workshops, I thought I had a handle on craft classes, whole class collaborations, the messiness that sometimes results in conversation about one student's work, or with my own plans as we discover some better way forward than what I had imagined. Within months of launching Blue Satellite Press, I realized the nature of our work and the challenges it presented weren't at all like the workshop-style teaching I had done. What was this type of class then? (See Table 10.1.)

Table 10.1   Nature of the course

Workshop	Studio	Internship	Apprenticeship
– Student work produced largely outside of class	– **Student work produced outside and during class time**	– **Student enters into existing enterprise**	– **One-on-one mentoring**
– Collective commentary/critique – frequent	– Collective critique – occasional	– Production independent of internship calendar	– **Shadowing** – Student performs preparation work
– Individual student work	– **Individual student work**	– Portion of production process (one of several tasks or portion of production time)	– **Non-formal, on-the-job instruction**
– Portfolio system	– Portfolio system		
– Learning ways of authorial intent and reader response	– **See work throughout the process**	– Isolated task(s)/job(s)	

I asked colleagues who supervise internships, internal and external, paid and unpaid. I asked nursing professors about how clinicals operate. I asked an art colleague about studio-style courses. I even leaned on my work experience as a carpenter's assistant over several summers.

As it turns out, the hallmarks and habits of most creative writing workshops were not viable options for a student-run publishing venture. It took me months to sort out, ultimately settling on a hybrid understanding of an apprenticeship and studio-style course. As a result, I teach the course differently now.

- I do more modeling, working as my students observe, then slowly transition them into greater and greater levels of engagement, introducing experienced, returning students as mentors and team leaders.
- Students work at their own pace – those intimidated by large machines might not feel as comfortable operating a letterpress, but ... the work goes on.
- We do not proceed until the work is sufficiently well-realized.

Because I was open to being a student in my own course, open about how to teach this unusual course to students new to every aspect of the content, and because I sought answers beyond myself and my discipline, I've found a healthy hybrid. Ultimately, the class taught me much about teaching in general: seeking new methods, looking beyond my own experience and expertise, looking beyond my own discipline, and responding to the specific needs of the course and the students in that course.

Listening to Customers

Being open to new ideas and listening to customer feedback are important entrepreneurial skills, so while teachers learn to teach student-run venture courses, everyone must learn to gauge customer response.

At one point, between broadside projects, Blue Satellite Press printed a fun greeting card and gave it a new imprint: Cheeky Greetings. The card proved fun to print and garnered some immediate attention and sales. So we've added more. Cheeky Greetings cards now number seven in total and they remain our most popular and most commercially successful item. Students listened to our customers and followed their instincts. The cards require a great deal of creativity, ongoing conversations about audience, and the same letterpress skills the course was designed to teach. What started as a way to keep the presses running during a lull has turned into an engaging and instructive part of the course.

ASSESSMENT

Profit Driven vs. Profit Assessed

Blue Satellite assumes a for-profit model: students engage the same thinking and market positioning as for-profit businesses. What products and services we offer, what print specifications (color passes, paper grade, etc.) we use, what price point we set all factor into the decisions we make about the projects. We factor projected modest initial sales against expanding inventory and a growing catalogue for growing future sales.

But a labor-intensive printing method has very thin profit margins. Letterpress printing has largely gone out of commercial use in part because of labor costs. So our English department has weighed the larger benefits of skill development, printing experience, and the practical and historical context for all our literature courses against the expectation that Blue Satellite support itself exactly as a private business. So, the successes of a course are not measured by how much money we make or by profit margins.

If profits aren't the measure of success, then what is? I've measured success in Blue Satellite by the following:

- Audience interaction. We've come to term this audience generally at Millikin as "third-party stakeholders." Sales (in dollars) are one way of measuring audience interaction, but so are other metrics: return customers, multiple sales (when one customer purchases more than one item at a time), the poets purchasing additional author copies. The poets themselves are third parties of another sort – their reaction to how we handle the process and the final showcasing of their work matters a great deal. We develop a reputation among poets as a press that handles them and their work with care, and we gauge our work alongside other literary publishers by the reaction of poets who have published in other venues.
- Improving and expanding the catalogue. Certainly, adding a quality print to the catalogue "improves and expands" what we have to offer. So too is the caliber of poet we choose to print. The press continues to garner interest and cache based on the quality of poetry we publish. In a similar way, the editorial tastes and literary aesthetics of the press reveal themselves in the ever-growing stable of writers, the range and consistency of those poets.
- Improving and expanding the quality of the printed work. Quality of the printed work is evident in the consistency of the print run, handling of ink and registration, the incorporation of new elements and new features in the prints (printing on angles or "in the round," reduction prints, etc.). So the new work is always adding some new element or skill to the prints we produce.
- Self-Sustaining. Yes, sales and marketing have been the weak link in the course, but the goals, by design, have been sustainability and engaging a writing and reading community. The press must cover its own material costs: ink, paper, etc.

Press Catalogue as a Collective Model

A great advantage for Blue Satellite Press with regard to assessment revealed itself slowly as the catalogue developed. Each new print improved on the previous print, and I was able to hold students to the quality of work achieved by their peers from previous semesters. The catalogue established the threshold for excellence. I didn't need to be the arbiter of excellence but the aid in achieving it.

Student models in many disciplines help to illustrate skillsets and high achievement. Those examples originate with peers (albeit from previous semesters), and so they operate on the level of students. Such student models, however, have an inherent excuse of exceptionalism – those models have been identified as extraordinary ones, the rare examples. The Blue Satellite catalogue, because it is a collective model, is not the exceptional product of any one exceptional student – it represents the work of all previous students, the neophytes and the returning experts, the students with ancillary skillsets (like graphic design students) and those with none at all.

Students see the previous work on display and some have expressed "I or We can't do that." The catalogue says otherwise – previous classes with the same demographics have looked at the catalogue and expressed similar doubts. Those classes have added quality work to the press catalogue.

Students' ability to work independently becomes an important barometer of their attentiveness and learning. Virtually everything in a letterpress print shop is new for the students, so I have to explain all aspects of the print process every term. The returning students enjoy the reinforcement of repetition and become adept, independent workers, some even developing a proficiency to lead a team of classmates. Not all student-run ventures rely on such antiquated, foreign industries as letterpress printing, so what I want to emphasize here is the hybridized nature of the pedagogy, one adapted for apprenticeship, studio-style courses.

Naturally, a course like this (a student-run venture, collaborative projects, 1–3 variable credits, students taking the course multiple semesters) creates some grading and assessment challenges:

- Students of different experience, skill, and comfort levels.
- Students with different levels of experience in this specific course, some returning a third, fourth, or fifth semester, others taking it for the first time.
- Challenges of balancing activities to run the business and assignments. Student-run ventures require forethought in creating assignments that align with the necessary operations of running the business. Some traditional classroom assignments might be useful (i.e., competition research that

takes the form of a research or response paper) for business development,
some are harder to align.

• The grey area of measures that determine a grade vs a component contribution to a larger class project. Group projects always present challenges for
grading: What has each student contributed? How much has each student
contributed to their designated portion? How much has the group had to do
to incorporate each student's individual contribution? How much has a high
functioning, ambitious student done to pull the weight of less enthusiastic
partners? Teachers have seen these and other related challenges again and
again. As I have said, assignment design can mitigate the uncertainties, but
inevitably some will remain.

Still, assessment of student learning necessarily has to happen. I was familiar
with the inherent challenges in grading creative writing courses: gauging
execution of craft, regardless of style; portfolio courses in which work is in
process all semester without grades on individual works, then revised for
a final portfolio. But the strategies I'd developed for these classes didn't seem
a good fit for Blue Satellite. So I asked colleagues, and the best suggestion
came from Sara Theis, a contributor here in the chapter on Pipe Dreams
Theatre. How does she handle all of the challenges I listed above? How does
she manage such a complex operation with a complete restart (new production
and new students) each semester? And how does she grade student contributions and assess student learning in such complex, shifting circumstances?
Simple answer: a midterm self-assessment. Each student at midterm fills out
a self-evaluation that looks very much like professor evaluations.

What I've come to learn is that students are exceptionally honest about
themselves, assessing their own effort, achievement, and learning. Given the
opportunity for quiet reflection, to see themselves objectively in a measure
specific to what they are doing and the course content they've committed
themselves to, students see themselves clearly where they are. This honesty
has held consistent semester after semester. This midterm self-assessment tool
has proven so useful that I now use it in all of my creative writing courses,
which do not have any formal grades before midterm.

Self-assessment is a reflective activity to see oneself relative to some set of
expectations or standards, either personal goals or the measures of a course.
So the habit of self-assessment and the necessary reflection it entails models
a habit of success, asking oneself:

• What did I want to achieve?
• What did I do to realize that goal?
• What did I expect as a result of what I did?
• What actually happened?

- What would I change about my actions to come nearer the goal? Or what did I learn that encourages me to revise my goal?

Student-run ventures rarely operate during scheduled class times, so another way to grade student work is their out-of-class contributions: attendance at events, set-up, marketing, "customer" interaction, communication with authors, etc.

Finally, another sure way of measuring student learning is their growing abilities to work independently at a task appropriate for each student's experience. No doubt, gauging their ability to work independently is a bit more challenging than the other measures, but it still proves reliable. Given the equipment and the assumed risk in operating it, I don't deny anyone help or explanation. Still, students become self-aware when I tell them, "I've shown this procedure to you three times. How about we do it together and you walk me through it, explaining what you're doing as we go." Under those circumstances, a student comes to know more clearly what she doesn't know, reinforcing what she does, and gains a bit of independence in procedures without realizing she is taking her first independent steps. And if she can explain to me what she's doing and why, she comes to know a bit of the enormous challenge and benefit of teaching: to teach something well, you often need to know something better or in a different way than you might otherwise.

All three of these grading or assessment strategies (self-assessment, out-of-class contributions, and growth in working independently) I've developed for Blue Satellite involve students self-monitoring, self-identifying in roles of greater responsibility and professionalization, a growth we want for all our students in all our classes, traditional or non-traditional, student-run venture hybrids. I mentioned earlier I have learned so much about teaching in general by struggling with the challenges of teaching Blue Satellite Press. The development of grading methods that actually help students rather than a separate assessment after learning has taken place – these have been among the most gratifying and important lessons for me as a teacher.

OUTCOMES

The primary goals for the Blue Satellite Press course are to give students (1) the courage to launch their own publishing enterprise, and (2) practice imagining ways to engage a writing community and a readership. Too many English literature and writing majors feel the dread of graduation: What now? They know the work they want to do, but how are they to do it? How can they pursue their interests and still pay their rent? How can they engage other writers when they may feel like an outsider or a newly published or even unpublished author?

Operating a press has put them in contact with poets across the country. It has given them an excuse to approach poets whose work they admire and spared them awkward introductions. More than anything, it helps bolster their confidence as they weather the early years of writing on their own.

Students gain editorial experience that helps to demystify the editorial process they may have known only as writers. As a result, they gain necessary perspective on their own work as it goes through the selection process at journals. They develop a keen eye in reading their own work from the perspective of an editor, effectively becoming better editors of their own work and revising more effectively. And they become better at locating venues for their own work, reading editorial tastes in publications and finding those that are likely to be receptive to what they are writing.

The following outcomes support the two primary goals, providing context for all English literature courses, frankly providing context for all humanities, liberal arts courses:

- knowledge of letterpress printing operations
- a sense of quality in letterpress printing
- knowledge of ancillary support: minor maintenance, cleaning, etc.
- history and importance of letterpress printing

How ideas are shared, who has access to those ideas, the great leap forward with movable type, the decentralizing of knowledge, the democratization of literacy – these achievements cannot be overstated. Movable type and letterpress printing that ensued for the next five hundred years is likely the greatest human invention. Gutenberg's great invention was not the printing press, it was movable type. Within one hundred years of the invention of movable type in the west (1450s), we see the seeds of every populist movement in Europe: religious, political, social, economic. This development happened as a direct result of decentralizing knowledge that followed in the wake of movable type. A publishing course of any number of varieties, and a letterpress printing course in particular, puts students in direct contact with that intellectual legacy.

CONCLUSION

The transition from student to professional, from learning to doing, is necessary and often fraught. Students are capable of more than they know and sooner than they realize. The sooner we facilitate that discovery, the sooner they can start imagining and realizing achievable goals. Students greet this transition with a look of surprise when they realize they have to be the doers, and then a delighted look of surprise as they make things happen.

Even if my students don't launch their own entrepreneurial venture when they graduate, I want them to learn entrepreneurial skills:

- self-management
- financing (not simply book-keeping, but funding, resource leveraging, and obligations)
- locating and soliciting expertise
- promotion – connecting work with audience

A student-run venture of any sort, any scale that asks students to provide vision, mission, strategic planning, craftsmanship, and execution sets students on an important path of discovery. When that venture is in their discipline, when it provides professional skillsets, when it models a life they are eager to live, when it introduces new, as yet unimagined ways of living that professional life, the experience is transformative, priceless.

Ideas for Teachers

Given the shortage of student-run ventures in English and humanities departments, I feel a commitment to offer suggestions for riffing on Blue Satellite Press (without having to acquire a 19th-century print shop) and for developing ventures in the humanities more broadly. In that spirit, I offer some ideas that are to varying levels affordable, sustainable, easy to launch, and full of the same wonderful challenges I discovered running Blue Satellite Press.

Because humanities disciplines are text based, and because my experience with student-run ventures has largely been publishing, much of what I suggest is print and publishing related. The advent of the internet has not decreased the consumption of written and carefully designed text – the internet has stirred the appetite for such things. For any publishing venture (print or digital), a software or design course is enormously useful. Such a course could provide computers and software (such as Adobe Creative Suite) or access to the ever-growing options of high-quality, free software (*Weebly* or *Word Press* for web design, for instance). Even without a course to give students basic skills with design and layout software, the venture itself could (as a credit-bearing course, a club, student activity) provide the necessary practice with such options.

If the goal is to launch a press, a publishing company of some sort, it will help to identify what exactly you plan to print.

- Books – requires funding and a more demanding model of profitability. Printing costs are often prohibitive. Robust marketing and sales are a requirement.
- Chapbooks/Pamphlets – these are by design and historical development more modest and less costly to produce, distribute, and sell. Of several

varieties, the least expensive of these are duplicated in the campus print shop in short runs. They have a high production value in layout, design and editing even if the printing is inexpensive. In fact, high quality design work can give a copier chapbook the look of a higher production value publication.
- Digital/Online – similar design work. Best vehicle for high design production are *Issu.com* or simply pdf copies.
- Website/Blog.

Publishers can take on any mission, any content they choose. A press that operates like a true university press will take on a considerable burden of ancillary operations: subject/content areas of specialty, panels of readers and peer reviewers, distribution, etc. And contracts with writers in many disciplines can be complicated and require promotions and events. As a demonstration of how the mission of a press can define the scope of the work involved, here are two examples that stake out very manageable identities:

- publisher of historical texts that are now in the public domain. Example: Lakeside Press
- publisher of literary works in the public domain. Example: Barnes & Noble Classics

Magazines afford students a venue for pursuing interests and expertise, cultural interests, and timely topics:

- locate art or music or literary scene
- cultural/language community
- food as vehicle for understanding culture, peoples: restaurant reviews, recipes, culinary skills and traditions

History departments might consider where they are as an opportunity to do the work of historical societies:

- local history in lieu of or in cooperation with local historical societies
- consultant for independent historical societies (Millikin's History department operated such a consulting student-run venture)
- historical repository (public/private records, corporate archives and records, particularly as businesses dissolve, industry archives that don't depend on any one company's proprietary archives)

Modern Language departments can think about writing and language services:

- language/translation services – liaison between customers and businesses, or business subcontractor

- language instruction/practice
- language and culture

If a collective single venture is too ambitious or a devoted course to operate it seems out of the question, smaller assignments in other courses can let students sample some of the fun and learning of business development. Ask students, for example, to develop their own press, a discipline-specific type of publisher, logo development, design of corporate package (letterhead, envelope, business card, promotional item) and pre-press design of a sample text. Any of the publisher models suggested above for any humanities discipline could give students a sense of the possibilities available to them.

perfor**M**ance
cons**U**lting

11. MU Performance Consulting

RJ Podeschi

MU Performance Consulting (MUPC) is a student-run venture that allows students to practice their craft as information technology (IT) and business professionals providing technical services such as web design and hosting, database development, and system analysis and design while simultaneously operating a consulting firm.

The venture was originally conceived by two IS (information systems) students as an independent study project related to IS and entrepreneurship. The two students saw the student-run venture as a way to sustain client projects completed in previous IS classes, and a way to provide additional real-world experience to students in preparation for the job market. One of the hallmarks of Millikin's upper-level IS classes was to work with a local client who had a specific technical need. Most are small businesses or not-for-profit organizations that don't have the technical expertise to perform system analysis and design work, web programming, or database application development. The two students asked, "What happens to all of the client projects we work on in class and who maintains them after the semester is over?" Their questions were in response to the way I incorporate real consulting projects into my upper-level courses, and they were spot-on. Students had been producing database applications and recommendations to clients, but when the semester was over, who was there to support them? In the real world, consultants don't provide a service and then sever the relationship with the client. They continue to support them after the engagement is over and work to build a long-term relationship. Why couldn't these student-led client projects work the same? From here, the client need was established and provided the catalyst to get additional support from Millikin's Center for Entrepreneurship to invest in this concept.

In 2014, the Coleman Foundation provided funding for me to infuse entrepreneurship into IS as a Coleman Faculty Fellow in Entrepreneurship. This fellowship was obtained through an application through the institution's Center for Entrepreneurship. Furthermore, this was the first fellowship granted to someone within the business school as technical disciplines are uniquely poised to ideate given the pervasiveness of tech start-ups within the last decade. Millikin's Center for Entrepreneurship is housed within the Tabor School of Business, but is really positioned as a cross-disciplinary initiative to integrate the entrepreneurial mindset into non-business disciplines. This student-led idea provided the basis for extending that fellowship; with training and financial support, to build the student-run IT consulting venture. In Spring 2016, a course entitled Technology Ventures was offered as an elective to build a feasibility plan for a student-run IT consulting company. Students performed customer research, built operational plans, developed an organizational structure, and worked with faculty to develop curricular requirements. The course was only offered once, but provided the canvas for students to drive how the new venture would function.

The student-run venture and one-credit course, Millikin University Performance Consulting, was officially launched in fall 2016 with six students, all of whom where IS majors. Students, through this for-credit experience, identify potential clients, enumerate requirements, provide estimates of work and cost, complete and test the technical work, and produce detailed documentation for knowledge transfer to the next group of students. Students utilize the Scrum agile methodology for organizing their work, are responsible for maintaining accounting records, managing performance metrics, engage in marketing and recruiting, and report to an advisory board. To date, the course has enrolled 36 distinct students (as the course can be taken multiple times), performed work for over 15 unique clients, and earned over $15,000 in revenue. The venture is now open to students from other disciplines in addition to IS majors to foster cross-discipline collaboration.

DISCUSSION

Let's face it, taking a business and making it fit within the confines of the academic world is a bit like putting a square peg in a round hole. Businesses don't have syllabi, they meet way more often than once per week, and the work doesn't come to a grinding halt in December and May. Based on the students' idea, I wanted to make the experience as much like a real work environment as possible. There isn't going to be someone telling you every single step to complete and much of it has to be "figured out" as you go. It can be messy and unstructured, and that's OK. It requires students to be self-starters, take initiative, and collaborate. Figure 11.1 shows a collaborative MUPC team meeting.

Figure 11.1   MUPC team meeting

> The one thing I found to be a distinguishing factor between the students was experience provided by internships. MUPC functions much like an internship in that the burden is on you to hold yourself accountable and take initiative. In this "class" there's not a teacher presence forcing you to come prepared and turn things in on time. (Former MUPC Student Consultant)

Not all client projects are perfect. Some are riddled with problems or may be outside of the comfort zone or skillsets of the student consultants. We had a client whom we had done work for in the past through multiple consultant projects through other courses come to MUPC for assistance in helping them extract data from their homegrown point-of-sale transactional system so they could convert to a new cloud-based system. Their homegrown system had a poor design that made data extraction difficult. Coaching students through this project was difficult. Students failed technically at times and also in communicating with the client. It was a strong learning lesson that you just can't replicate in a traditional classroom. Students had to be focused on getting it right; that there was something at stake. Doing work that was "just good enough" may get you a degree, but it won't meet the client's needs and expectations.

> I think the best thing about being in a student-run venture is how it allows you to fail fast and learn from the experiences. For me, I think one of the biggest takeaways

was simply working with a real client, facing real problems and coming up with a solution. The experience students gain from being in one of these ventures is the closest thing they will get to real life work experience. One big difference between a student run venture and the classroom is the overall environment. You're not just focused on completing assignment after assignment making sure you come out with a good grade, but having a real product to work towards. The value that a student-run venture gives students, and gave me, is priceless. MUPC gave me the first glimpse of what it looked like to work in my profession, and I am grateful for that. (Former MUPC Student Consultant)

In the end, it's about providing students an opportunity to test drive the skills they learn in the classroom in an environment that is as close to their first job as possible.

I hoped to exercise what I had learned in the classroom despite my lack of industry experience, and that's exactly what I was able to do. Millikin provided an umbrella under which I could spread my wings. At a time when minimum wage positions in the food service and retail industry were my only options, the student-run venture provided a realistic environment to exercise my skill set safely while still learning about the implications of running a business. (Former MUPC Student Consultant)

ASSESSMENT

The student-run venture was designed as a one-credit course that could be taken multiple semesters. This was done intentionally so that students could build competency and leadership while bringing consistency and institutional knowledge to the venture. Students perform technical services for existing clients which were previously started as real-world client projects from other IS courses. In addition, students seek new business from clients in the community and on campus. Students gather requirements, provide an estimate for services, a time line for completion, and manage each project end-to-end. They are ultimately responsible for the success and failure of each decision they make. I serve as a liaison, buffer, and safety net for students as needed. When a project is complete, students have the client sign-off on the work and present them an invoice to be paid. Students pay themselves an hourly wage for work on client projects. All finances go through the university and students are paid through the university payroll office. Students reserve 50% of the prior semester's net profit for reinvestment into the venture. Their reinvestment can be spent on technology, conference travel, or wages to lead specific business-related projects.

The university assumes some level of risk knowing that students are performing work for external clients under the institution's name. All students sign confidentiality agreements at the beginning of the semester, and again with each individual client. In addition, students have language for documents such as scopes of work and project sign-off reviewed by in-house legal counsel. A year-end report is provided to the university's Center for Entrepreneurship on clients served, and financial statements are submitted to the university business office on a regular basis. In addition, the advisory board provides a forum for students to gain additional advice and expertise beyond the faculty's point of view. Between the faculty, the Center for Entrepreneurship, and the advisory board, there are sufficient checks and balances to ensure that students can experience real risk and real reward with a safety net in place.

In the original course design, enrollment was limited to IS majors. However, as roles became more defined and skill assessments were performed, it became apparent that a diverse set of disciplines were needed in the venture, just as is common in a typical organization. In 2018, the venture opened up to students who have taken Foundations of Information Systems, a course required by all business students, because majors outside IS are allowed to take the course. A typical semester has between 10 and 14 students enrolled. Each class meeting begins with a venture-wide Scrum, led by student leaders, to address the current status of client or business-related projects, set tasks for the next week, and address any roadblocks. Students are "coached" each week by the faculty during the later portion of class time and address timely topics specific to the client or the business operations. These topics can include, but are not limited to: learning the consulting process, working with difficult clients, budget forecasting, code review, or managing DNS. Guests with specific strengths are sometimes invited to help students work through acute problems.

Students begin as junior consultants in their first semester and are promoted to associate consultants the following semester (assuming a re-enrollment) after learning the operations and taking ownership of a specific process or task for the semester. This could be anything from taking meeting minutes to managing email and social media to building and maintaining the office computer equipment. Associate consultants work on client projects and perform operational functions for the venture. I will appoint two or three senior consultants to lead client projects and operations of the venture for the semester. These are typically students who have been in the venture for multiple semesters, have internship experience, and have previously demonstrated leadership and organizational qualities. Senior consultants often continue as senior consultants if they elect to enroll again in a subsequent semester, but can be rotated out due to changing needs or poor performance.

We typically meet formally once per week for an hour. During this time, senior consultants lead the group in an agile Scrum session to answer three key questions: (1) what have you worked on in the past week?; (2) what problems/obstacles have you encountered?; and (3) what do you plan on completing by next week? This structure allows everyone on the team to see the big picture and the details simultaneously. It also allows me to assist with problem solving or running interference when technical or client issues arise. The Scrum session can take anywhere from 15 to 25 minutes depending on the work load. The other time is used to cover specific topics of interest. For example, I typically lead a class discussion on consulting practices, and the entrepreneurial mindset each semester, but have built-in technical sessions as well. In addition, I will also bring in guest speakers from the community or the advisory board to provide a different perspective and a forum for conversation. One of my continual concerns is that if I'm the coach, I am the only voice they hear. Students need to be exposed to a variety of ideas and thoughts to shape how they want to run the venture.

While some client projects can be completed within the bounds of the academic semester, some continue from fall to spring or from spring into the summer months. Initial conversations with potential clients include time line requirements, and expectations related to response time, communication channels, and milestone objectives. Even though students earn credit for the course, they are also paid for their work. As a result, students will continue working on client projects when school is not in session with faculty supervision. Even though they aren't earning credit, they are still being paid for their work, so there is still an element of motivation there. Students have the ability to turn down a prospective client due to unclear objectives, too large a scope, unreasonable time line, or if the client's project does not fit within the skillsets of the consultants.

Because the venture is dependent upon client work and can vary greatly from semester to semester, student consultants are evaluated in the course through means that mimic a workplace more than a classroom. Student consultants are charged with developing a set of goals for the semester. These can be technical in nature, non-technical such as verbal communication, or organization-related to advance a new initiative for the venture. Students must determine how they will measure their success in each of these goals, and report at the end of the semester, using both quantitative and qualitative methods, on how they met (or did not meet) their goals (Table 11.1 is the template we use). Similarly, students go through two performance evaluations; one at midterm and one at the end of the semester. Students complete a self-evaluation and the faculty completes the same evaluation. The self-evaluation asks students to rate themselves (on a scale from 1 to 5), in the areas of communication, job knowledge, work habits, quality of work, problem-solving ability, initiative, attitude and cooperation, adaptability, and leadership ability. Additionally students are asked to write a one-page narrative summarizing their performance and engaging in reflection. One-on-one meetings lasting approximately 10–15 minutes take place to compare the evaluations, provide constructive feedback on how to improve, and provide a forum for the student consultant to voice any concerns. Student consultants also complete a team evaluation to rate the

Table 11.1   Performance objectives

Semester goal	Performance measure	Status	Indicated change to improve performance
Example: Improve customer service skills	**Example**: Satisfactory rating or higher from client and team surveys	**Example**: Survey not administered, to date; however, feedback from co-workers indicates I need to be more empathetic	**Example**: Place myself in others' shoes, spend more time listening, seek feedback on progress from others
1			
2			
3			

Table 11.2   Kolb's elements of experiential learning

Kolb's required elements of experiential learning	Evidenced through student-run consulting venture
1. Include a concrete experience	1. Work on real-world client projects and perform business operations
2. Include abstract conceptualization	2. Requirements gathering, forecasting, project planning, and strategic thinking
3. Include active experimentation	3. New business models, different ways of tracking project progress, using different technology tools, and performance testing
4. Engage in reflection	4. Performance evaluations, Scrum meetings, and client sign-off sessions

quality of work of their peers. Student consultants report to an advisory board at the end of each semester, and occasionally reach out to them for mentorship throughout the school year.

From a pedagogical perspective, this student-run venture exemplifies two specific active learning frameworks. These include Kolb's (1984) work on experiential learning, outlined in Table 11.2, and Merrill's (2002) first principles of instruction for effective and efficient instruction related to active learning as seen in Table 11.3. Kolb's learning theory, specifically, combines experience, perception, cognition, and reflection to create knowledge through experience; all hallmarks of real-world projects. Merrill's principles of instruction focus on the knowledge transfer from existing knowledge or new knowledge into the student-run venture, or in this case, creating an environment similar to that of a consulting practice.

Table 11.3   *Merrill's first principles of instruction*

Merrill's first principles of instruction that learning is best achieved when	Evidenced through student-run consulting venture
1. Learners are solving real problems	1. Student consultants are performing real work for real clients, handling payments and expenses. They are running a business.
2. Existing knowledge is activated as the foundation of new knowledge	2. Student consultants use knowledge gained from previous courses (technical and non-technical).
3. New knowledge is demonstrated to the learner	3. Some projects involve skills not yet learned or practiced.
4. New knowledge is applied by the learner	4. Student consultants select how business is transacted, and how work is completed for clients.
5. New knowledge is integrated into the learner's world	5. Student consultants document their work into a knowledge base for current and future student consultants.

OUTCOMES

Over the past four years, students have earned over $10,000 in revenue and served 15 unique clients. Some of those clients return each semester for new projects or ongoing work. A profitability summary can be found in Table 11.4. The course has enrolled 36 distinct students with a total enrollment over six semesters of 69 students. The maximum number of semesters a student has been enrolled in the venture is four, while the average tenure of a student consultant is 2.03 semesters. As is the trend in technical disciplines, the gender balance skews towards male (80.5%) over female (19.5%). The student-run venture benefits from a diversity of majors with the following participating: Information Systems (22), Digital Media Marketing (4), Mathematics (4), Accounting (2), Entrepreneurship (1), International Business (1), Music (1), and Theatre (1). Some majors like entrepreneurship and digital media marketing, as well as the entrepreneurship minor, require at least a semester in one of the 14 student-run ventures on campus, so this provides a forum for those students to experience work in the technical space.

Student consultants have completed projects for clients that involve web design, network consulting, server/system implementation, database programming using Microsoft Access, data migration from Postgres to a cloud point-of-sale application, system analysis, design and recommendation, web application development in WordPress and Vanilla Forums, and mobile application development using PhoneGap and Microsoft PowerApps/SharePoint. In general, students gain client projects through word-of-mouth or actively seeking new work through their existing network of connections. In fall 2018,

Table 11.4   Financial summary

	2016–2017	2017–2018	2018–2019	2019–2020
Revenue	3,095	3,423	2,626	1,584
Expenses	3,134	4,554	1,248	1,783
Profit (Loss)	(39)	(1,311)	1,378	(199)

student consultants recognized the majority of their client work was web related. As a result, they decided to begin offering web hosting and support services and acting as the intermediary between the client and a third-party hosting provider. Students promote this as a value-added service to clients who don't have the expertise or interest in managing a website. Additionally, students manage all the financials using QuickBooks Online and coordinating deposits and checks through the university business office. They track projects using Trello and physically on a white board full of sticky notes. For communication, students use Slack with different channels for each client and have preferred it over traditional means such as email and group texts.

For the last four semesters, fall 2017 through spring 2019, students completed a team evaluation of their peers. Within that peer evaluation was a section asking students to rate on a scale from one to five, one meaning never and five meaning continually, how often they practiced certain skills in their particular role of the venture. Within this collection period, 33 team evaluations were gathered. The skills ranged from technical to functional disciplines such as accounting and marketing, but also included essential skills like collaboration and presentation. In summary, 87.9% of students recognized that they practiced communication and collaboration either often or continually, project management (69.7%), and consulting (51.6%). System analysis and design is being practiced, in some form, by at least half the students (51.6%). However, 72.8% of students self-reported that they practiced technical skills either never or barely, accounting (66.7%), and legal issues (66.7%). When looking at the data set in totality, it becomes apparent that somewhere between 18% and 25% of students are working either in a technical or business discipline with a defined role, while between 39% and 70% of students are practicing essentials of communication, presentation, consulting, entrepreneurial thinking, and so on. The data show areas where students may need to be paying more attention such as legal risk and may also indicate that those working on technical projects may be individuals and not teams of student consultants. Furthermore, it may be concluded that either the majority of the technical work is being completed by the minority (rather than the majority) of student consultants or that the student consultants perceive some work as not being technical (e.g., system analysis and design, research and recommendation, web content updates). However, upon further reflection, it may very well be that a technically-related student-run venture is simply a vehicle for practicing critical skills such as: communicating with clients and teammates, understanding a client's problems for solution development, and developing and following through on a project plan.

> The work I did in student-run ventures helped me land my first internship and then later a job out of college. The experience in leadership and the various examples I was able to give for every scenario that an interviewer had questions on all correlated directly to experience with MUPC. Most of my work was focused directly on customer-facing projects. This was extremely beneficial, as it gave me the experience I needed to work with end users. My first job out of college was web-app development. Everything around that job is working to create a customer's vision. My work through courses and MUPC at Millikin gave me what I needed to handle that job in stride. (Former MUPC Student Consultant)

Students across all the disciplines mentioned above reflected in their evaluations on what the experience provided for them. Multiple IS majors stated that they learned how to work with clients better while increasing their technical skills on-the-fly rather than from a textbook. Additionally, students commented that the student-run venture forced them to learn and adapt as situations and requirements changed. One IS major said "I believe it gives me a huge step ahead with my major and learning how to deal with real-world clients will be important in my future internships and jobs." Another IS major learned that "you can't always rely on email to communicate with individuals, and that sometimes you must use alternate methods like phone calls or physically visiting them." Math majors who were interested in IS commented that the experience provided them with more collaboration and team work than what was typical in their discipline. A digital media marketing major said "I worked continuously on trying to better understand how to market the student-run venture to our multiple target audiences and ways to engage our followers while sharing information about the business. This aspect of the business really showed me that you can't just post a picture on your social media that you find relevant and expect people to engage with it. You have to post eye catching pictures that followers want to see and create opportunities for them to engage." In general, students have had positive experiences from the student-run venture while preparing them for careers in their chosen disciplines.

CONCLUSION

Starting and running a student-run venture admittedly consumes time from the faculty's perspective. In lieu of preparing for class lectures and grading typical work, the time is spent gathering progress reports from students, and following up with clients, if necessary. In general, it has been my perspective to engage with the client at the onset of the project and at the completion so that the student consultant must manage the process in the middle. The faculty solicits feedback from the client throughout the project and only intervenes when problems occur. It has been my philosophy to act as a coach rather than a dictator. It's their company and it needs to be driven by them, the student consultants. The senior consultants are the ones to take charge and direct the student-run venture on how to operate. Again, the venture is meant to be "faculty-led" and "student-driven." The faculty advisor is there as a safety net, but at the end of the day, students need to take ownership of their decisions, whether they are good or bad, reflect on them, and make recommendations on how to enact change.

Ideas for Teachers

It's critical that a student-run venture be driven by students from the ground-up, and that you allow the students to evolve the venture over time. The value of letting your students drive the entire process is critical. It should also be noted that it took two years to bring entrepreneurship to the IS discipline, which allowed for ideas and the mindset to incubate. Students had to see the vision; I couldn't be the one to tell them. It took another two semesters to prove that it could be successful. My mindset was also to let this grow organically. It allowed for the risk appetite of students and the institution to be tested incrementally.

> As a co-founder of the business, I went in with an in-depth understanding of what the business would entail. That being said, I was in a unique situation where I helped design and run the business from the ground up. Something that most students didn't have with existing student-run ventures. I got to actually see my business take off and the struggles that came with it. I'd also like to add that a lot of the ideas we had going in were NOT the results, and the business has changed tremendously in the few years that it has been alive. I think that surprised me the most. I knew we wouldn't think of everything, but a lot of the things that changed were the ones we thought were core to the business' foundation. (Former MUPC Consultant and Co-Founder)

This experience works well for students who are highly motivated and interested in taking initiative. Developing a system for allowing high-quality students into the venture is an important aspect of ongoing success. In this particular case, it has worked well for current students to recruit new students into the venture. They oversee vetting and interviewing students to recommend for invitation, and are ultimately signed into the course by the instructor. Having proper evaluation instruments in place for checkpoints throughout the semester also provides a way to deliver corrective action for those who are under-performing.

As students work on projects for a client from semester to semester, it is imperative that students build documentation of their work for future student consultants. This is a challenge in the professional workplace, and it remains a challenge in this student-run venture as well. Not only are student consultants required to document their work, they are required to teach someone younger than them about the project. The two methods reinforce sustainability and strengthens the knowledge of the student consultant who worked on the project. Although students manage a Google Drive account for convenient access to files and data from the cloud, a dedicated office space is helpful to have for students to work on projects that require specialized software, to meet with clients, or to collaborate.

Additionally, students need to be given the opportunity to improve existing processes such as billing or social media or client communication. Part of working on the business and in the business concurrently is applying the entrepreneurial mindset of finding ways to do work better given the resources available while recognizing new opportunities. Students need the autonomy and permission to develop new streams of revenue, new markets, or research and develop their own IT solutions. Overall, the student-run venture has provided and will continue to provide students opportunity to practice their disciplines in a real-world setting with real risk and real reward.

REFERENCES

Kolb, D. A. (1984). The process of experiential learning. In D. A. Kolb, *Experiential learning: Experience as the source of learning and development*. Upper Saddle River, NJ: Prentice Hall.

Merrill, M. (2002). First principles of instruction. *Educational Technology Research and Development*, 50(3), 43–59.

12. Blue Connection Art Gallery

Kate Flemming

One of the more unique student-run ventures at Millikin University is a retail art gallery, named Blue Connection after the school's mascot Big Blue. Unlike the majority of student-run ventures, Blue Connection is located off Millikin's campus, enabling it to become part of the Decatur arts community. This has allowed the gallery, which was one of the first student-run venture courses created at Millikin, to establish relationships with the Decatur Area Arts Council and other neighbors in downtown Decatur, Illinois.

Since the opening of Blue Connection, the gallery has moved several times. Blue Connection currently rents space in the Madden Arts Center, adjacent to the Decatur Area Arts Council galleries and offices. The location offers two floors of gallery space, 770 square feet in the main gallery and another 1,000 in the basement, 350 feet of that space is usable gallery space, and the remainder is available for art storage.

As a consignment gallery, inventory consists of art created by current students, alumni, art faculty, and friends of Millikin University. The gallery offers a generous consignment rate of 70% to current students and 60% to alumni, faculty, and friends. The value of the consigned art on hand varies throughout the semester and academic year, with the highest amount I observed while instructing the course being nearly $50,000. While technically under the non-profit umbrella of Millikin University, the course is presented as a for-profit business model to students.

The hallmark of the Blue Connection gallery is the After 5 Live exhibit openings, which coincide with the downtown First Friday Gallery Walks, where featured artists interact with the community and give brief talks about their work. During these events, the majority of Blue Connection art sales take place. The gallery also takes advantage of other arts-based community events in the downtown area, including:

- Arts in Central Park Juried Art Show each September, which presents more than 60 exhibiting artists from several states
- Holiday Walks and special hours each December
- Pop-up art shows

The gallery is also the location of the summer Robert H. Crowder Artist-in-Residence program. Each year, a current student or recent alumnus of the Millikin art program is chosen to complete a 6-week residency at Blue Connection. The resident keeps regular hours and uses the gallery as a studio. At the studio, the community is welcome to stop in to talk with the artist about their work. The resident generally hosts 1–2 exhibits during the summer and is also the September After 5 Live featured artist. While there is no course for students to run the gallery in the summer, the artist-in-residence gets a unique experience, and the gallery benefits from the sales of their artwork. The 30% income from summer sales helps cover necessary expenses when it would otherwise lose money.

As a student-run venture with a physical space, Blue Connection has overhead costs. The largest and most important expense is its rent to the Decatur Area Arts Council. Each year, Millikin University covers the rent expense for the gallery. In doing so, it allows students to focus on reaching a break-even point or profit tied to their chosen vision for the gallery. The second-largest expense is cost of goods sold, an expense paid to artists, accompanied by sales tax payments. Remaining expenses include phone, internet, duplicating charges, booth fees, etc. associated with gallery activities. Most expenses are out of the control of students, including internet and phone, which are inherited and necessary costs.

Students in Blue Connection are not paid for time spent in the gallery. Hours spent running the gallery are equivalent to the hours expected of a student to work outside of course meeting time. Students in the course are expected to cover all operating hours at the gallery, or in special circumstances, work within their budget to arrange for coverage. Schedules and hours are established each semester as a team. Students are also required to schedule adequate coverage of special events, including the After 5 Live events.

The primary source of revenue for the gallery is income from art sales. There are some instances where students have procured non-sales-taxed revenue (say

Table 12.1   Blue Connection curriculum integration

Area of study	Required	Credits
BA in Art	Capstone – Required	3
BFA in Studio Art	Required	3
BFA in Art Therapy	Required	3
BFA in Graphic Design/Computer Art	Required	3
BS in Digital Media Marketing	Suggested Course	1–3
BS in Entrepreneurship	Suggested Course	1–3
Minor in Entrepreneurship	Suggested Course	1–3
BA/BS in Arts Administration	Suggested Course	1–3
BA/BS in Arts Technology	Suggested Course	1–2

a sponsorship or selling a shelf or stand that is no longer in use), but this did not occur during my time teaching the course.

My first semester teaching Blue Connection was in the Fall of 2016. At that time, the gallery had been in existence for 13 years, and many resources and equipment had been accumulated. In the main gallery, there were vinyl-based floors with replaceable sections, self-healing walls (a major investment in 2011 to upgrade from a time-consuming hanging system), and a POS system and software. In the basement, there were shelving and displays, a large inventory of art, cleaning supplies, and more. On the administration side of the business, there was a bank account with a checkbook, artist contracts, and paperwork. Resources of support across various academic and non-academic departments on campus were already in existence: business office, information technology, art department, and business school, to name a few. This structure made it easy to navigate impediments as a faculty member, and also made student questions easier to answer. As already mentioned, the support of the community and proximity to other arts spaces and events only helped us accomplish students' goals for the semester.

Blue Connection is variable in credit (1–3 credits) and cross-listed in both Entrepreneurship (ET390) and Art (AR390). As of the 2019–2020 Millikin University course catalog, Blue Connection is a required course or a suggested option for required credits in many disciplines. Table 12.1 provides a breakdown of where and how Blue Connection is integrated into the Millikin Curriculum.

The group of students running Blue Connection at any given time is a collision of expertise, most often with students from the arts and business concentrations. This chapter will focus on my experience teaching the course during Fall 2016, Spring 2017, and Fall 2017, with emphasis on the last semester. At that time, the trend was for students to take the course just once for 3 credits.

Within this model, the course was likened to a "drinking from a firehose" experience – instantly immersive and fast-paced.

DISCUSSION

The objective of the Blue Connection student-run venture course is for students to advance the entrepreneurial concepts of opportunity recognition, assembling resources, customer awareness, and risk assessment.

Upon completion of this course, students will be able to:

- Recognize and develop business opportunities
- Assemble human, financial, intellectual, and material resources to execute business opportunities
- Assess and develop strategies to mitigate risk associated with business opportunities

The focus of the course is on creativity and innovation, as each specifically relates to the growth, development, and operation of Blue Connection. Creativity and innovation lead to successfully achieving a balance among artist, customer, and gallery – creating value for all parties. Figure 12.1 depicts the interrelatedness of artist, customer, and gallery.

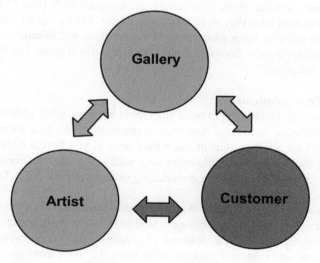

Figure 12.1   Successful balance of artist/customer/gallery

Table 12.2   Blue Connection Gallery team options

Management	Marketing
Inventory Acquisition	Social Media Marketing
Creative Merchandising	Traditional Marketing
Building & Grounds	Copywriting
Gallery Coverage Schedule	Customer Development
Event Coordination	Overall Communication
Artist Contracts	

Audience engagement and associated teamwork needed between students for value to be created proved to be my biggest challenge as an instructor. Here are some excerpts from my syllabus during my first two semesters:

Roles

Instructor
It is the instructor's job to create a challenging environment worthy of the futures Millikin students will build upon graduation. It is not the instructor's job to make the experiences of this course easy. When challenges arise, it is the instructor's responsibility to allow students to find opportunities for illumination such that those who have been involved with Blue Connection will be more than what they were when they began. The instructor will mentor students so learning takes place from both successes and failures – both are honored as experiences from which students can and will grow. The Instructor is not the "Manager."

Gallery Team (students)
It is the Gallery Team's job to meet challenges head-on, work collaboratively and communicate needs and outcomes. Remember, when you spend a little extra time with a fellow student when they need it, you have a better chance of getting them to spend a little extra time with you when you need it. Each student will participate in either a marketing or management team. Table 12.2 depicts each of the teams.

This process simply did not work for me as an instructor. In my Spring 2017 course, art students and business students did not work together, and it was obvious. There wasn't a "collision of expertise" that created value for the artist, gallery, and customer. Instead, there were collisions from siloed groups that were not communicating or working together as a team.

There were some wins, however. The flyers produced by a student in the course were some of the most impressive pieces of graphic design I had ever seen. Unfortunately, these flyers were not delivered before the deadline or posted in enough time around campus and the community to promote the show. Despite my best efforts, I wasn't able to guide them into better teamwork.

The biggest and most frustrating challenge I experienced was the lack of commitment of some of my classmates. I took pride in the ownership of our business and was disappointed by the disinterest and lack of passion some students displayed. (Sydney Doherty, Fall 2016)

Some challenges range(d) from minor obstacles all the way to seemingly impossible tasks. Some challenges consisted of struggling to delegate tasks among students with individual schedules. Another challenge was allowing the professor to step down as the leader for us students to take their place and oversee the business. (Adam Macke, Spring & Fall 2017)

It was at the end of the Spring 2017 semester that the agile philosophy of working and scrum framework for project development were introduced to me. Agile originated in the software development industry. The agile manifesto declares:

We have come to value:
- Individuals and interactions **over** processes and tools
- Working software (or working "product"/"prototype") **over** comprehensive documentation
- Customer collaboration **over** contract negotiation and
- Responding to change **over** following a plan

That is, while there is value in the items on the right, we value the items on the left more.[1]

This was the mindset I wanted to see from Blue Connection students. I noticed that my business students tended to place value in the items on the right, and my art students tended to place value on the items on the left. As a result, I began my summer of 2017 developing a new syllabus that utilized the scrum framework to enhance the creative teamwork of my students.

The terms agile and scrum are often used synonymously, but it's important to understand their correct use. Scrum is a way to put agile values into practice. A person is agile, but they perform scrum. Scrum is a framework within which people can address complex adaptive problems while productively and creatively delivering products of the highest possible value, and within which various processes and techniques are employed.

So how can scrum be applied to a retail art gallery student-run venture at Millikin University? I return to the overarching goal of the course: to successfully achieve a balance among artist, customer, and gallery – creating value for all parties. For my Fall 2017 syllabus, I merged these definitions together:

> You are a part of a high-performing, cross-functional team. You will have to creatively deliver products (in whatever "form" that may be) to create the highest possible value for the artists you represent, the customers you serve, and the gallery you own. The scrum framework will support the communication, accountability, and transparency within your team, allowing you to make the creative, entrepreneurial decisions to execute your vision of the gallery's growth for the semester. Much like the many other tools you will acquire during this course, your proficiency in the scrum methodology will add value to any future collaborative, entrepreneurial endeavors you encounter.

Scrum Framework Implementation

As I mentioned, there was not "a collision of expertise" between business and art students. I knew my students had the knowledge and skills to create value, but the siloed management and marketing teams were not allowing individual members to shine.

Roles

Scrum promotes gathering a team of "T-shaped" individuals. A "T-shaped" individual is one that has a depth of skills or expertise in a single area (the vertical line) as well as abilities in or potential to collaborate across disciplines (the horizontal bar). Individuals may have more than one area of deep expertise, and the breadth of their other various knowledge and skills could be numerous. Scrum teams are self-organizing and cross-functional. They own "how" the work is accomplished because it is the combination of their knowledge, skills, tools, and time that is necessary to complete a sprint – or length of time – of work.

In the first meeting of Blue Connection, I brought paper and art supplies and asked the students to create their "T" and share with classmates. Julian Gutierrez, a business student, shared that he "likes to talk" and is not afraid to strike up a conversation. It made us chuckle, but one of the successes during the Fall 2017 semester were video interviews with the artists that Julian produced with his classmates. He used his strengths to collaboratively produce videos that created value for the gallery and artists.

There are two additional roles within the scrum framework: the scrum master and product owner. In a classroom setting, the instructor takes on the scrum master role. Scrum masters are best defined as servant leaders responsible for ensuring that scrum is understood and enacted within the organization. The scrum master serves the team by guiding them in removing impediments, facilitating scrum ceremonies, and helping those outside the team understand

Table 12.3   Scrum framework

Scrum Framework		
Roles	**Artifacts**	**Ceremonies**
Team Members	Product Backlog	Sprint Planning
Scrum Master	Spring Backlog	Review
Product Owner	Product Increment	Retrospective

how their interactions contribute to or hinder the scrum team's ability to produce work.

Beyond helping my students understand this new tool (scrum), the servant leader, or "guide on the side" mentality, is what is needed from an instructor of a student-run venture. Solidly placing myself in this role gave me the ability to help students think through their decisions, facilitate better feedback and communication between the team members, and advocate for them to the community and campus.

The product owner pulls together the vision for a product, gathers input from external parties, and clearly expresses backlog items. Different from the team members, the product owner owns "what" work is being done, keeping an eye on priorities that need to be accomplished. Students that feel confident in their ability to look at work in this broad manner continuously provide feedback to their peers and professionally interact with outside parties for input.

The optimal size for a scrum team is six people, plus or minus three. Scrum, in its essence, is a small team of people that is flexible and adaptive. As I will soon discuss, we had many "products" that the team worked on throughout the semester, and it was required that a minimum of three people work together on each product. Table 12.3 illustrated our scrum framework.

Artifacts

The vision for a product or service is the starting point of the scrum framework. From the vision comes the roadmap – an evolving plan that will change as more is learned from customers, the market, or other factors. Then, the product backlog, which is a comprehensive list of all the things that need to happen for the vision to be accomplished, is created. The product backlog will evolve, but at the beginning, it is filled with everything known that needs to be done. This list is prioritized by the highest risk and/or value of the item.

In our first meeting, I explained the scrum framework and gave the only "homework" assignment of the semester. Each student was given a Sharpie and Post-It note pad and asked to write as many tasks as they could think of that needed to be done before our First Friday Gallery Walk the following week. The next time class met, we went through everyone's thoughts to create product backlogs.

It was then time to plan our sprint, which is where a product is completed of the highest possible value within a fixed period of time. The first step in sprint planning is deciding how long the sprints will be. I chose that our sprints would be weekly. A sprint should be short and never longer than 4 weeks. Shorter iterations uncover opportunities for improvement, and sprints are repeatable. To create the sprint backlog, items are pulled from the top of the product backlog and discussed with the team. Items are pulled and discussed until the team indicates that enough has been placed on the sprint backlog to accomplish during the week. During sprint planning, the team determines *how* the work is going to be accomplished – breaking down items into specific tasks. Finally, the team members self-select which tasks they want to complete for the sprint. Figure 12.2 depicts a sample sprint board.

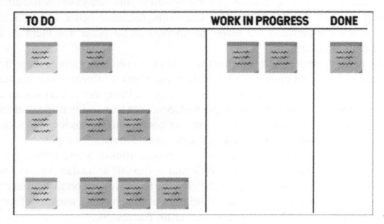

Figure 12.2   Example sprint board

Throughout the sprint, team members move their tasks from "to do" to "work in progress" to "done." In the gallery, we had about 4–5 boards simultaneously being completed, including upcoming show needs, marketing, and inventory management.

Ceremonies
At the end of the sprint, the team will have produced a minimum viable product (MVP). What this MVP looks like varies based on the product backlog. The MVP could be a marketing flyer, artist interview video, or review of inventory, but it is complete enough to review and discuss the progress of the work.

The review is a show and tell opportunity for the team with any external parties to share their *progress*, the "what" they accomplished. External parties can interact with the MVP in a way that is meaningful to them, and a way that gives feedback to the team while it's still relevant. The review is an important meeting for the product owner, as she is diligently listening and taking notes that will ultimately modify, rearrange, add or subtract items from the product backlog for the next sprint. The review is the only ceremony where external parties can give feedback. For Blue Connection, those parties included representatives from the Decatur Area Arts Council and Millikin art faculty.

After the review, the team holds a retrospective, facilitated by the scrum master. In this meeting, the team discusses their *process*, "how" they accomplished their work. Both ceremonies lead to continuous improvement, with the outcomes from the review informing the product backlog for the upcoming sprint and the retrospective identifying improvements to the team process before the next sprint planning meeting.

Incorporating ceremonies into our scheduled class meeting time made the time together significantly more productive. Students were held accountable for their work. They came prepared to share their progress and discuss their process. As they grew more comfortable with the framework, they led their own planning and reviews. This schedule still allowed us to have time to be in the gallery together, enabling me to be a servant leader, guiding the students with their creativity and innovation to grow the gallery.

ASSESSMENT

Assigning a grade in a student-run venture is not an easy task. Since teaching this course, I have seen grading methods of colleagues at Millikin University and at other institutions that I would have tried in Blue Connection. However, I was happy with the following evolution of my assessment to accommodate the inclusion of the scrum framework.

The first areas of assessment were ones the students had the most (or complete) control over.

Class Attendance & Participation (150 points): Two excused Wed/Fri class absences are allowed before it impacts the grade. After two excused absences (or for any unexcused absence during the semester), each absence will result in a 50-point deduction from the final grade.

Class attendance was mandatory, as it was the time for students to review their progress and process together. I included the following definition of "excused" to my class:

> Notifying Kate directly of your absence before the class meeting. I understand that there are life events we cannot control and discretion will be used in a fair manner.

Many students have jobs and other obligations or responsibilities. As long as the obligations weren't extremely personal, I made students share with the class why they would be missing a class period. If a student had more than two excused absences, we discussed in class what they were doing to make up for it (so as not to have the 50-point reduction). This transparency worked. And more often than not, students needed to miss class for things like interviews or special activities with a student organization, and their peers wished them good luck and celebrated their success.

Daily Standups (150 points): Daily standups are mandatory and have many options for completion. Much like a "homework assignment," they are either completed or not. There are no make-ups for missed daily standups.

Daily standups are an additional ceremony in the scrum framework. Students had 100% control over their daily standups. We utilized the project management software Basecamp as a virtual meeting space. Each day, the students were pinged to submit their daily standup, which included three questions:

- What did you do yesterday?
- What are you doing today?
- What are any impediments you may have?

Much like an email message, students could attach images or documents to share. Basecamp has the social media function of tagging others. A standup may look like the following:

Yesterday I finished the flyer (see attached). Today, @John and @Jane could you proof? No impediments.

Through using this software, I was able to see what students were accomplishing each day. If there was an impediment that needed my guidance, I was able to engage with students immediately. Each standup was worth 2 points, which was a small amount, but they add up over time. Standups would also signal to their classmates that they were or were not completing their work and contributing to the team's success. If a student wasn't posting, it was noticed and pointed out.

After 5 Lives & Other Gallery Events (200 points): After 5 Live events are mandatory, and absences from these events (and others) must be excused, and effort must be made up through special projects. If they are not made up, all points will be forfeited, and up to 100 additional points may be lost. The instructor has discretion based on overall effort and performance.

If a gallery event was missed, much like class attendance, students shared ways they were going to make up missed attendance to help with the event.

On-Site Gallery Hours (250 points): 50 points will be deducted for each on-site gallery session missed. If there is a conflict, the student must find coverage. If coverage is found, then no points will be deducted. Whoever covers the on-site hours will receive 20 extra credit points.

This could easily be renamed "Customer Engagement Hours." Everyone must work in the gallery at some capacity. Even if it's just 1 hour a week, each student needed to have a chance to interact with customers and understand the operations of the gallery. To prevent gaps in coverage, extra credit points were awarded to students who cover for a peer.

Final Reflection (100 points): A final reflection paper is required to ascertain the depth of experience and level of understanding achieved throughout the course.

The final reflection included a self-assessment of the student's experience in the venture. First, they provided a paragraph describing behaviors they personally observed in themselves as a part of the Blue Connection. The behaviors reflected upon were: tenacity, passion, tolerance of ambiguity, creativity, self-belief, flexibility, risk-taking, and control/ownership.

Second, they described three experiences where they learned from interactions with artists or customers, and analyzed how the behaviors and actions of:

1.   the artist impacted the customer and gallery,
2.   the customer impacted the artist and gallery, and/or
3.   the gallery impacted the artist and customer.

For the final part of their reflection, each student wrote a paragraph answering and elaborating on the following:

*   Identify and describe your favorite part of the Blue Connection experience. Be specific. It can be an event or any element of the experience (teamwork, financial reporting, setting up, cleaning, marketing, etc.).
*   Identify and describe your least favorite part of the Blue Connection experience. Again, be specific.
*   Describe the greatest lesson you personally took from this experience.
*   What is something you will do differently in the future, and why?
*   Examine the final income statement for the semester. What recommendations would you make for next semester?

The second areas of assessment were not as easily controlled by an individual student. Feedback from their peers, customers, and artists was taken into consideration.

Team Member Evaluations (300 points): Team members will evaluate the participation and engagement of each other.

This assignment was the midterm for the semester. Each student had to rate and give constructive feedback about their peers. The assignment also asked students to pick just two peers to hypothetically open up a gallery with, and explain how the two peers complemented their own strengths and weaknesses. After I received evaluations, each student scheduled a meeting with me. I did not share the full evaluations with the students, but I did share their average rating, as it was factored into their midterm score. The final grade for the midterm is the average rating from their peers combined with the grade I assigned from the quality of their own completed evaluation (did they complete it, provide all that was asked, use correct spelling and grammar).

Financial Goals Presentations (150 points): Financial goals for each event and a summative goal for the semester will be mutually agreed to by the team members and instructor. Weekly financial goal presentations are mandatory, with no make-ups.

For about the first month, I modeled the financial presentations. The students are taking in so much all at once that making sure we discuss financials is a major win. But once they became comfortable with the POS and began to connect the dots between the sales and vision for the gallery, I assigned pairs of students to lead the weekly discussion. If they did not prepare and lead the discussion, the points missed affected the whole class.

Customer Evaluations (100 points): Customer evaluations will be requested and collected throughout the semester to determine the quality of customer service at Blue Connection.

During the semester, I had several secret shoppers visit the gallery and complete a survey. Survey areas included cleanliness of the gallery, friendliness of the students, clarity of signage and information about the artwork, and ease of their transaction (if they purchased an item). Each student received the average rating from the customer surveys for these points.

Artist Evaluations (100 points): Artist evaluations will be collected to determine how well artists believe they were represented at Blue Connection this semester.

The artists also completed a satisfaction survey. Survey areas included cleanliness of the gallery, the quality of the interactions with the student team, the marketing of their show and artwork, the timeliness of their payment, and the overall quality of the representation they had from the gallery. Like the customer surveys, each student received the average rating from the artists' surveys for these points.

Finally, if all expenses were covered (other than the rent expense paid by the university) and a positive net income was achieved, Gallery Team members would receive 100 points of extra credit, which would raise grades by up to a whole grade.

OUTCOMES

Blue Connection was unlike any other class that I have ever taken. Kate didn't feel like a professor but a boss that respected you in the workplace. Everything is very hands on, what you make of it, and holding yourself accountable when it came to things like setting up for the shows, bringing your ideas to the table and opening up the shop during the week for regular hours of operation. Being in Blue Connection my last year of college, took away the nerves of entering the real world and prepared me for whatever job came my way. (Julian Gutierrez, Fall 2017)

Scrum is founded on empirical process control theory, which asserts that knowledge comes from experience and making decisions on what is known. Three pillars uphold every implementation of empirical process control:

- Transparency, meaning all aspects of the process must be visible to those responsible for the outcome
- Inspection, meaning all visible aspects of the process should be inspected frequently enough to detect undesirable variances, and
- Adaptation, meaning if any aspects have deviated outside of acceptable limits, the process must be adjusted to compensate.

This excerpt from the Scrum Guide perfectly sums up the benefits of its value-driven teamwork:

> When the values of commitment, courage, focus, openness and respect are embodied and lived by the scrum team, the scrum pillars of transparency, inspection, and adaptation come to life and build trust for everyone. The scrum team members learn and explore those values as they work with the scrum roles, events, and artifacts. Successful use of scrum depends on people becoming more proficient in living these five values.
>
> People personally commit to achieving the goals of the scrum team. The scrum team members have the courage to do the right thing and work on tough problems. Everyone focuses on the work of the sprint and the goals of the scrum team. The scrum team and its stakeholders agree to be open about all the work and the challenges with performing the work. Scrum team members respect each other to be capable, independent people.[2]
>
> *I was surprised at the amount of creative control that I and my fellow classmates were allowed. I had expected to be involved in the decision-making process but my expectations were exceeded by how little restrictions were placed upon the execution of our plans.* (Adam Macke, Spring and Fall 2017)

My Fall 2017 class achieved a small profit that semester, which was a rare feat in the venture's history. After working hard to promote artists and gallery shows, the class had the final opportunity for sales during the holiday season. On the Friday of finals week, I popped in to the gallery. I can still remember the look of excitement on the faces of my two students as I walked in. A man had just purchased a sculpture, priced over $300, which was much more than the average sales amount. Making the sale even more impressive was the fact that this sculpture had been in the gallery inventory for several years. A post was made in Basecamp to let everyone know of their success, and everyone received 100 points extra credit.

CONCLUSION

Pedagogically, my greatest challenge was creating an experiential classroom for creative and effective teamwork to thrive. However, there are even more challenges to instructing an off-campus student-run venture, including:

- Being on call 24/7 for any issues at the gallery.
- Acting as a bookkeeper for the venture.
- Understanding and even updating the technology used, including the POS system.
- Maintaining community relationships and the understanding that the classroom is a laboratory.
- Monitoring the social media accounts for the venture.

The course is an experiment for the instructor, too, and we experience failure every day. The scrum pillar of transparency was integral in my servant leadership of the course, as I had to be honest with the progress of my responsibilities. I believe that my students understood that I was putting in just as many hours as they were to help them succeed in their creative vision for the gallery. Figures 12.3–12.5 show the physical space Blue Connection occupies and we invite you to explore the gallery on your next trip to Decatur, IL.

Figure 12.3   *Front entrance of Blue Connection Art Gallery*

Figure 12.4   Blue Connection Art Gallery interior wall

Figure 12.5   Blue Connection Art Gallery interior space

Ideas for Teachers

1. *Don't be afraid to experiment.* Incorporating a framework from the IT industry seemed scary, but I have had many past students reach out to me and say that they have either encountered it in the workplace and were glad they knew what it was, or they used it for their own personal artistic projects. Not every tool we tried to add to their toolkit resonated, but that does not mean that it was not worth introducing.
2. *Use a growth mindset as you test your venture.* Establishing strong partnerships and resources can help take the burden off you as an instructor. In a larger community, a creative based co-working space or co-op gallery could be a good off-site partner, and might reduce overhead costs and worries.
3. *Understand your university's financial protocol.* I can't overstate how important it is to understand how to make the financial aspect of your venture work with your institution. There is a lot of front-end work that needs to be done, and your administration and staff are some of your most important and valuable resources.

NOTES

1. https://agilemanifesto.org/.
2. The Scrum Guide by Ken Schwaber and Jeff Sutherland. © 2017 Scrum.org and ScrumInc. Licensed under CC by SA 4.0. https://www.scrum.org/resources/scrum -guide.

MILLIKIN

Café

13. Arts Café

Mark Tonelli

Resourceful entrepreneurs can recognize opportunities and take advantage of them. Arts Café, a live performance venue student-run venture, was created out of recognizing an opportunity. Millikin University has a venue for nearly any type of performance you could possibly imagine. There is a large theatre for theatrical productions, a medium-sized theatre for scaled-down productions, and a recital hall for chamber music concerts. However, before Arts Café, there was no intimate, "artsy" space for students to enjoy late-night events on campus.

Off-campus, there were and are a handful of bar-restaurants that have small stages for performers. But after 9:00 p.m., these venues are closed to patrons under 21, and at an institution with primarily undergraduates, this means most students have no place to see live performances in an intimate space later in the evening. The idea to create a space for small performances for audiences of all ages on campus was born.

In 2016, Millikin hosted the Society for Arts Entrepreneurship Education (SAEE) national conference. One session left a permanent impression on me – a panel of current and former students who had enrolled in the student-run venture Pipe Dreams. Running the theatre was shaping the careers of current and former students in profound ways. I attended a Pipe Dreams show during the conference, and I was blown away. The level of professionalism given to all aspects of the show was beyond impressive. The artistic director – a student – introduced himself to me before the show. Then, before the curtain rose, he previewed the season for the audience, just like at a "real" theatre. I then enjoyed a well-executed show, artistically and technically, all accomplished by students.

I found the idea of a student-run venture, a course and business operated by students, fascinating. As my idea for an intimate on-campus venue intersected with the student-run venture concept, the idea crystallized. This would be the way to realize it. In turn, I pitched the idea to colleagues and students, and they were excited. This gave me the confidence to pursue it.

Arts Café is now a one-credit course and student-run venture open to students of all majors and years without prerequisites. Though it resides in the School of Music, because a music professor teaches it, Arts Café is offered through the Center for Entrepreneurship.

As a Coleman Fellow, I received start-up money to fund the new student-run venture. After receiving start-up capital for the café, it was time to start putting in the work to create the course and recruit students. I asked colleagues to invite students to participate in a pilot course called Arts Café. I also invited students I thought would make good candidates for the course and made a presentation to the entire freshman class of the College of Fine Arts, from which I garnered a great deal of interest. Around 40 students showed interest in the idea, and 20 joined on to create the initial core group of students for Arts Café.

The pilot course met each week for two hours during the semester. Determining how to use this time was challenging. There was no syllabus, which felt liberating at times, and other times, terrifying. The course began to unfold, and the not-for-credit pilot proved to be successful, and the Council on Curriculum granted approval for the course to be offered for credit. Arts Café has now been offered for-credit for seven consecutive semesters.

DISCUSSION

The work involved in operating Arts Café is divided into five core areas or "teams," including Artistic Direction, Entertainment Management, Marketing, Accounting, and General Management.

Artistic Direction: The Artistic Director oversees all employees of the student-run venture and executes on the overall vision for Arts Café.

Entertainment Management (EM): The Arts Café brings in acts to perform on-stage. The Entertainment team identifies and recruits artists. From the moment artists make their initial contact until they pack up their gear and head home after a performance, the EM team guides them through the process.

Marketing: The Marketing Manager and team raises local awareness of Arts Café through traditional and digital media to "put bodies in seats."

Accounting: The Accounting team manages Arts Café's finances, which includes creating a budget, managing ticket sales, and tracking all expenditures and revenue.

General Management: The GM and team manage logistics. At the shows, the GM ensures everything runs smoothly.

In addition to the five core areas of work, additional tasks often arise, and students are quick to jump in and take on any additional responsibilities. This allows me, as the professor, to observe from a bird's eye vantage point. In a traditional sense, I am the owner of Arts Café – I "own" the idea (though as noted in Chapter 4, the university is the true owner of Arts Café, a fact which is downplayed so that students feel empowered to engage in running the business). Like other business owners, I trust the responsibility of running the business to others – in this case, the students. They make all the decisions. It is my responsibility to assist by pointing out blind spots they may be missing, which is another way I provide instruction.

Teams are comprised of 2–3 people, led by a manager. All five managers form the executive board. The Artistic Director is the leader of Arts Café – the students' boss. Each team manager reports to the Artistic Director, and additional team members report to their respective managers. Figure 13.1 depicts the streamlined reporting structure for Arts Café. This structure has helped student leaders run the venture in an efficient manner.

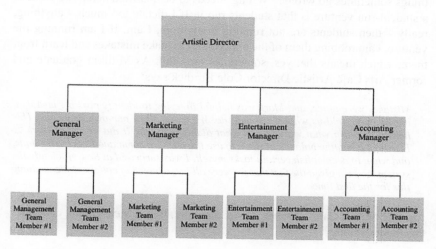

Figure 13.1   Arts Café reporting structure

Students are put into teams through an interview process led by the Artistic Director. This process is a good example of how Arts Café ideally functions as a completely student-run venture. Yet teaching a course that students run presents pedagogical challenges. It took some time to partition class time effectively. Eventually, I settled on the "bookend method." The first few minutes are for academic announcements. Then, the Artistic Director takes over and runs a 40-minute business meeting. During the last few minutes, I jump back in with observations or recommendations about the students' discussion, but I never dictate the course of action. The students make all the decisions, which I believe is key in student-run ventures.

I rarely lecture in Arts Café. I may train teams or students to help them learn their jobs, bring in a variety of guest speakers related to Arts Café's work, or ask students to research their job online or interview a professional who has their job. Otherwise, students do everything. This paradigm can be disorienting to students accustomed to the teacher leading instruction. As Shawn Daniels, a Millikin graduate and one of Arts Café's former entertainment managers says, "[Arts Café] is very different than many courses I had taken at Millikin because more hands-on had taken place and I was able to live through my work and practice, learn and teach others in many fields of work."

You may be asking, "But if students do everything, and I don't get involved, can't things go wrong?" I have been asked this question several times, including at a conference where I presented about Arts Café. The answer is yes, things sometimes go wrong. "Wrong" needs to be qualified here. The point of a student-run venture is that students run it. If I dictate too much – anything, really – then students are not running it anymore, I am. If I am running the venture, I am robbing them of the opportunity to make mistakes and learn from them, which means that yes, sometimes they fail. As Millikin graduate and former Arts Café Artistic Director Cole Burdick says:

> *Mistakes were made, and Mark was helpful in trying to identify possible mistakes, but he never told us what we should do. We made all of our own decisions. This helped us learn what worked and what didn't, and why it did or didn't work ... I learned a healthy balance of when to use the chain of command to get tasks done, and when to accomplish certain tasks myself. I was surprised at how efficiently the system worked, given the fact that we were all just a bunch of college students doing this for the first time.*

Another of Arts Café's former artistic directors, Becca Mendenhall, continues this theme, noting:

> *At a live show, it takes practice, but you have to be able to make decisions on the fly if problems arise in order to solve them, because as they say, the show must go on ... [S]tudent-run ventures ... [give] students the opportunity to get professional*

experience under the umbrella of their institution, and better prepare them for the real world. I wasn't really sure what to expect when I first got involved in Arts Café ... [Since enrolling] I know I personally learned who I am as a leader, and I have been able to work on my own personal skill sets through various opportunities.

Students, working together, will not make every possible mistake, but they will have had enough failures and successes to learn to think strategically. In turn, I see Arts Café as a laboratory. I encourage students to take calculated risks. Arts Café is a business that students are charged with running, and it cannot continue if it is completely run into the ground. Positive growth is the goal, so there is always a delicate balance of enabling students to be creative while charging them to be responsible with their creativity. While students are encouraged to make a profit, there is no requirement to do so. Students are instead made aware of the unavoidable impact of financial decisions on a business.

The "Arts" in Arts Café

Arts Café's mission statement says: "Millikin Arts Café is an entrepreneurial endeavor run by the students for the community. Our goal is to provide an artistically eclectic environment in which artists of all creative arts can come to showcase their talents." Figure 13.2 shows an Arts Café performance.

Figure 13.2   Arts Café student performance

"All creative arts" and "eclectic environment" are key pieces of Arts Café's aesthetic. While the course is offered through the School of Music, and I am a music professor, Arts Café is not a music course, and as a venue, Arts Café is not a venue only for "bands." Arts Café has featured dance troupes, comedians, rappers, poets, chefs, and a one-man show. Therefore, "arts" truly expresses the range of art forms Arts Café encompasses. As I say to students, "if something can be done to a high degree, then it can be considered an art."

As mentioned, Arts Café is a 1-credit elective open to students of all majors without prerequisites. Students are encouraged to take the course for consecutive semesters. Several students in Arts Café have stayed with the venture from the beginning of the pilot phase. Others have enrolled every semester it has been offered for credit. This creates continuity and institutional knowledge, as continuing students help train incoming members on how to run the business.

Students majoring in music, theatre, business, arts technology, entrepreneurship, and the humanities have enrolled in Arts Café. This interdisciplinary mix is important. Students learn to see "how the other side lives" as they work together with people from other fields. In this sense, Arts Café models the highly interdisciplinary nature of work in the 21st century. Students learn the value of the network other students bring to the table. They learn that it is as much *who* you know as *what* you know.

The Performance Space

Before it becomes Arts Café at night, the performance space is a stage in the corner of the cafeteria in the University Commons. Students transform this space into Arts Café. While this takes time, it allows students to exercise their creativity.

Transformation begins with the Arts Café "look." Pipe and drape black curtain, string lighting, and the student-designed Arts Café logo comprise the backdrop. Around 10–12 tables are rearranged to form venue seating, covered with tablecloths and candle centerpieces, and the overhead lights are dimmed. The effect is indeed intimate and has a unique look compared to other performance spaces at Millikin. This look is part of the "branding" of Arts Café.

Arts Café is a venue, however, Arts Café is not restricted to one space. Occasionally, the company holds performances in other spaces. For example, Arts Café produced an Earth Day concert outside on the university quad. A Halloween party, "Big Boo Bash," was held in one of the university's banquet rooms. Holding a show outside the performance space is a carefully weighed decision. A strategic number of shows outside the performance space can create a certain novelty, but too many can dilute the brand. If too many shows occur outside the venue, patrons may become confused about what Arts Café is and lose confidence in it as a venue.

As any business begins to mature, additional opportunities develop. An unexpected by-product of self-producing events has turned into a side business. Arts Café now produces other organizations' events. For instance, the university tasked the College of Fine Arts (CFA) with developing a celebration for the dedication of the University Commons building. Knowing Arts Café's ability to produce high-quality shows, the Dean of the CFA asked Arts Café to produce the event. The event was successful, and Arts Café has since been asked to produce several more events. Recently, Arts Café worked with a student to produce her senior capstone project.

As a self-sustaining venue with its own in-house marketing, general management, and entertainment management teams, Arts Café can contract out a wide range of professional services. These services have the potential to generate more revenue than Arts Café's own events. A benefit of providing professional services is that they require far less time and resources than producing an Arts Café show, resulting in a favorable work-to-income ratio. As an example, during a semester, Arts Café partnered with a local off-campus venue to host different Millikin performing ensembles each week. In this capacity, the professional service was "talent booking," and Arts Café's entertainment management team booked artists into the off-campus venue's space. Initially, students had questions about its feasibility:

- Is weekly too frequent?
- Would monthly be more manageable?
- How will taking on this job impact Arts Café's ability to operate its own venue?
- Are the artists getting paid, and if so, how much?
- Will Arts Café get paid for providing this service?

These are representative of the types of questions students discuss when considering a new opportunity – weighing the human and financial resources required to manage outside opportunities and how it will impact their ability to manage the core business.

ASSESSMENT

Activity in Arts Café does not exist linearly – there is no straight line to accomplishing work. Arts Café exists in multiple layers that intersect in different ways, from the physical business itself, to the abstract concept of Arts Café, to assessing the students' work academically. Layers collide and repel unpredictably. There is a definite, yet desirable, messiness in the nested roles of a business that is a for-credit course.

I maintain a hands-off approach and truly allow the venture to be student-run when possible. But if the students run the business, then what do I as the teacher do? Well, in addition to ensuring professionalism in all areas of the business, I assess the students' work, employing two overarching modes of assessment: running the business and academic assignments.

Running the Business

The quality of students' work in operating the business is important, and their grade depends heavily on how committed they are to the business. Do they actively participate in class meetings? Do they fulfill their jobs at events? The general management team has the responsibility to handle logistics, but mounting an event often requires all hands on deck, so everyone in Arts Café receives a job at an event.

Most students tend to take jobs seriously and pull their weight, but not every student does. Some hide in a corner when they should be sweeping the floor or hanging stage curtains. Some students arrive late or leave early, which are both red flags. I have had a couple of "no shows," which the syllabus explicitly states are unacceptable. This is because the crowning work of Arts Café is its events. The course is, after all, about running a venue. If students do not attend the events in the venue, then they cannot "run" the venue, evaluate planning, gauge the quality of an event, or determine what can be improved in the future.

I have found non-arts majors more than arts majors tend to struggle. Perhaps this is because arts majors are more accustomed to having class during the day and having practices, rehearsals, and performances at night. Business and humanities majors, on the other hand, may find this new territory challenging. Their idea of a class might be restricted to "class meetings." With a student-run venture, however, much of the work happens outside of class meetings, and it can take time for non-arts majors to catch on. Nurturing and extra training or instruction with non-arts majors to help them acclimate to the arts world is an important step to take for the business, but this must be recognized by the students.

The flip side is that arts majors sometimes become enamored with grandiose ideas without considering how to accomplish them. Non-arts majors can have a tempering effect on the arts majors, drawing out the practical side and bringing them back to earth. The idea is not to squelch dreams. On the contrary, I encourage students to dream big. But the reality is that dreams require tangible support to realize them. This is where a business major can help an arts major think through the "financials," that is, the feasibility, of how to accomplish the dream. The reverse can sometimes also be true – some artists inherently consider the fiscal implications of their ideas, while business-minded students are clueless about how impractical certain ideas are. Ideally, regardless of their place on the arts-business spectrum, both the artistic and business side of each student develops as they engage in the work of Arts Café.

Table 13.1   Arts Café budget for "Sundae Fundae" event

Sundae Fundae Budget Snapshot
Tickets – $3 ahead of time, $5 at the door, $27 revenue from ticket sales
Supplies – $54 (ice cream, toppings, bowls, spoons, napkins, etc.)
Payroll – $0
Rental Fees – $0
Door Gifts – Millikin Arts Café Stickers
Net Profit: –$27

Table 13.2   Arts Café template for purchasing supplies

Template for purchasing supplies
1. Use what supplies Arts Café already owns,
2. If the supplies Arts Café owns cannot be used as is or modified to fit the theme of the show, then borrow supplies, and
3. If no organization or individual is able to lend supplies, then purchase the supplies.

Arts Café events typically have a small budget. From a recent semester, Table 13.1 shows the budget snapshot from an Arts Café show, Sundae Fundae, which focused on culinary arts. It featured an ice cream bar from which patrons could make their own creations and Millikin's executive chef, Brian Pehr. Pehr gave a talk on his career and a 6-minute healthy cooking demonstration in which patrons entered a raffle to eat Chef Pehr's meal.

The ticket prices for this show are fairly standard for an Arts Café show. Patrons are incentivized with a less expensive ticket ($3.00) if they purchase ahead of time.

Supplies for this event were a bit on the high side, even at $54, because most of Arts Café's events require few additional supplies beyond sound equipment. Occasionally, Arts Café produces a show that requires "themed" or specialty supplies, as was the case here. In general, Arts Café follows a three-step pattern when considering what supplies it needs for a show, as shown in Table 13.2.

Organizations are sometimes quick to purchase supplies before considering what they already own or can borrow. Because Arts Café earns modest revenue from its shows, it needs to compensate on the front end by keeping costs low. Using or modifying existing supplies or borrowing supplies is one way to do that. When Arts Café determines that the best course of action is to purchase supplies, it searches for supplies that can be purchased cheaply. Dollar Tree has become Arts Café's best friend! It is surprising what can be found at deep-discount stores that will work quite effectively for an event.

In terms of payroll, Chef Pehr donated his services, as is often the case. Arts Café generally only pays performers when they are not Millikin students or faculty members. Since there was no live music for this show, no rental fees were incurred. Some shows require rented sound reinforcement equipment, which can cost as much as $100. Gifts given out to attendees at the door are stickers with the Arts Café logo on them. Arts Café purchased 1,000 stickers for $50 and has either used the stickers as giveaways (as was the case here) to promote the organization or has charged $1.00 for them at some events. Naturally, with $54 in supplies and $27 in ticket sales, Arts Café lost money.

The money "lost" ($27) is negligible and hardly felt, particularly with a reserve from Coleman funding. What is gained, however, is likely of greater value: the opportunity to produce a new type of event (culinary arts) with some interesting twists. The students in Arts Café could not recall seeing such an event previously. They strategically plan events that differ from others around campus, even events of the same type. In turn, the financial loss is outweighed by the buzz created from the event and perception that Arts Café produces "cool" events, which ideally encourages greater attendance and correspondingly greater profits in the future.

Academic Assignments

Since Arts Café is primarily hands-on, it becomes important that students connect with their learning by writing about it. Typically, there are 5–10 written assignments per semester. Assignments from a recent semester included:

1. *Work Plan.* Each team member will design a work plan for the semester using the Work Plan template. This will include outlining the specific duties of the team member's position, identifying problems to be solved that are unique to the venture at that moment, and establishing deadlines for accomplishing the solutions to problems. This can be done in one or two pages.
2. *Training manual.* Each team will either revise or create a training manual for their team, using as many pages as required – no less than two but probably no more than five.
3. *Live event performance paper.* Each student is required to attend one non-Millikin arts performance, which includes music, theatre, dance, poetry, performance art, etc., and write a paper discussing its relevance to the operation of Arts Café. This project is two pages.
4. *Resume.* Each student will create a resume of their education-related and professional accomplishments, and include a detailed section that describes their duties in Arts Café. The resume is typically one page.

5. *Reflection paper.* Each student will write a reflection paper evaluating their overall effectiveness in accomplishing their duties, proposed solutions, and deadlines outlined in their Work Plan in 2–3 pages.

6. *Peer evaluations.* Each student will evaluate the effectiveness of all other students in Arts Café. Instructions for completing this assignment will be given in class. The Artistic Director will also evaluate team members twice during the semester.

Most of the assignments are 1–2 pages, primarily because students are completing the majority of their work while running the business. Yet, even simple assignments can be valuable. For example, I hand out peer evaluations early in the semester, which allows students to see what their peers will hold them accountable for, and what they will hold their peers accountable for. This document can help focus and direct the students' work. The peer evaluations then serve as a type of rubric, providing a yardstick for students to measure the quality of their work.

In addition to written assignments, the entire class has one collective, culminating project, which is a final impact presentation to the "board of directors." The board is comprised of Millikin faculty members from across the university who I ask to serve on the board solely for the students' final presentation. The students' job is to make an accounting of Arts Café's growth over the semester. Each student is required to have a speaking role in the presentation. The board's job is to listen, ask questions, and evaluate the quality of the presentation on a written form.

OUTCOMES

The learning outcomes for Arts Café state the following:

> Students will gain greater confidence in understanding the intricacies and roles entailed in operating a live performance venue. The skills learned in these roles will help students identify their passions and interests and apply them as performers and entrepreneurs to their careers. Their understanding of the dynamics at play in interacting with performers, industry professionals, administrators, the public, and other stakeholders will enable them to better navigate the world of live entertainment and its related social and economic factors.

A key phrase is "identify their passions and interests and apply them as performers and entrepreneurs." The first part of this phrase focuses on learning about business ownership, meaning Arts Café is designed to accomplish at least three things:

1. Expose students to the world of business ownership.

2.   Help students decide whether it is for them.
3.   If they decide it is for them, then apprehend corresponding skills.

Some students discover that they do not want to run a business, and they self-select out for the future. Others discover a passion for it, and Arts Café gives them a taste of business ownership, confidence, and helps them develop skills.

   This leads to the second part of the phrase – apply skills "as performers and entrepreneurs to their careers." Arts Café deals with the arts world, and in an overly simplistic sense, it can be divided into two broad categories: artists and industry personnel. Artists create art; industry personnel provide infrastructure. If students enrolled in Arts Café pursue a career in the arts, they will likely fall into one of these two categories. Either way, the skills they develop in Arts Café will serve them well.

   For instance, if a student pursues a career as a performer, then she will have learned critical processes for creating her own employment opportunities. She will understand that certain venues cater to certain types of artists. She will learn to identify a person who books talent. She will learn to develop an appropriate marketing campaign. She will learn to consider stage set up, sound reinforcement, ambience, and interaction with the audience. She will learn all these things, because she will have participated in making it all happen multiple times behind the scenes in her own venture at Arts Café.

   Even though she may not be in the show, she is learning through observation how to successfully conduct a performance, artistically and financially. Artists do not always know where to begin or what questions to ask. Arts Café gives them a framework. It helps students learn what questions they need to ask and how to ask them. From this starting point, they can begin the process of producing their own events and gradually build their careers. Students in Arts Café with an interest in being professional artists will learn to help themselves instead of feeling helpless or solely relying on others to decide if they are worthy of stage time or making a living in their craft of choice.

   Similarly, if a student pursues a career on the industry side, they will have learned all the same things through the lens of someone in a support position. They will have learned what the issues are, and how to help artists succeed despite the challenges they face.

   As one of the newer student-run ventures at Millikin, Arts Café has few former students who have graduated and can reflect on how the venture has influenced their careers. To understand how current students feel Arts Café *will* impact their careers, I asked them. Specifically, I asked them to list three things they learned in Arts Café and to explain how those things would help them in their careers. Their responses are divided into five themes (I have edited some responses for clarity):

- Teamwork
- Time management skills
- Running a business
- Communication
- Leadership

Teamwork

Because Arts Café is divided into five teams, the concept of teamwork and working with others was a common theme. Responses included "working with a team," and "it's about the team," or simply, "teamwork" and "unity." Other responses begin to uncover certain issues, like "[y]our team is only as good as your weakest player."

An interesting response was, "don't trust in your [team]mates, they'll probably want to [work less than you], and being dependent [on] someone who [doesn't] work can lead you into not doing your own work properly." The notion of trust emerges frequently in Arts Café. As they work together in teams, students begin to form opinions about the quality of their team members' work. Some students become disgruntled, feeling that their team members do not share the same dedication to the cause and are not performing up to their capability. Depending on how the manager or team members handle them, issues of trust can be like a cancer. If they are caught early and addressed properly, they can heal and strengthen the team, but if left unaddressed, they can eat away at the team, creating suspicion and eroding the team's ability to function. Ideally, the manager is proactive in setting a vision and expectations for a team, and addresses issues if things go awry. Some managers, however, are uncomfortable approaching someone about a problem, and they let things go, hoping the problem will just disappear naturally over time. It usually does not, and this is when the team begins to implode.

My approach is to alert the Artistic Director and recommend that she speak with a given manager to resolve issues. This way, I enable students to address issues themselves and confront and resolve difficult situations. I have occasionally broken this rule. I've learned over time that breaking this rule results in students becoming dependent on my solving problems for them rather than solving them for themselves. In turn, they learn nothing. Again, teaching a student-run venture requires restraint by allowing students to fail, even when you see failure coming.

Time Management

This theme is not necessarily a surprise with college students, who frequently struggle with time management. In multiple responses, however, students cited that running a business, with its many tasks, helped develop their ability to manage time. One student in a management position told me in a private conversation that the heavy workload in Arts Café was the one thing forcing him to be organized in all areas of his life.

Running a Business

Running a business can be an eye-opening experience for students. I hear many variations of "I didn't know the amount of work that goes into a business" and "running a venue is not as easy as it seems." One sub-theme is the concept of failing, as in "how to successfully (and unsuccessfully) run a business." Even when failure does occur, as one student reflected, "that's ok, because we learned from our mistakes and fixed it for next time." Sub-themes of resilience and flexibility also emerged, as in, "many times we have to make last-minute changes to an event or plan. Being able to think fast, recover, and come up with a solution to the problem is a skill that is valuable to every career."

Communication

This theme emerged frequently, primarily because students tended to discover that breakdowns in communication led to negative results. A common scenario entailed the students getting excited about booking a certain artist for an upcoming show. The Entertainment Management (EM) team would contact that artist with an initial inquiry, but then the students would get busy attending to other aspects of planning the show, and forget about the artist. In the meantime, the artist would not get back to the EM team. As the date of the show neared, the students' big artist was not available because the EM team had not stayed on top of recruiting them. Inevitably, the students would then have to scramble to find a replacement artist, which was not always possible. In turn, these types of scenarios may have elicited the following responses:

"I cannot prepare things at the last minute."

"The minute we lose focus is the second our plan starts to become not as strong."

"I learned appropriate times to follow up if you don't get a response, requesting things with a deadline so people don't forget what you're asking for, etc."

"It is so important to thoroughly communicate all details, not just 'important' ones … Communication is also best when it's further in advance."

"Being able to communicate could make or break a job opportunity."

Leadership

Multiple responses touched on leadership skills gained in running a business, particularly for those in management positions. For example, "If I am ever in the position where I have to lead a team of people or run an event for an organization, I learned effective ways to manage groups of people," and, "Being in a leadership position ... taught me to figure out how to lead new people and work through unfamiliar situations while having people looking to me for guidance." Some students were more philosophical: "I found more of who I am as a leader, how I lead, and preferences I have in a professional sense." Students also learned that good management involves delegation: "... it will be incredibly beneficial to know how to delegate tasks effectively. If you can delegate well, you will always be able to meet your deadlines."

There were also some isolated responses that did not form a theme. One is worth noting – "sales." This is a curious response because Arts Café does not sell a physical product; it sells an experience. Yet students may come to recognize that any business requires an element of salesmanship, whether that means selling tickets to an upcoming show and not being "afraid of 'coming on too strong'" when approaching a potential ticket-buyer or creating a social media post that "catch[es] the eye aesthetically."

CONCLUSION

Reflecting on Arts Café's development and progress, I am acutely aware of my inadequacies in teaching it. Twenty-five years of on-the-job experience as a self-employed musician – booking gigs, leading musical ensembles, and writing and selling arrangements, textbooks, and CDs – has involved a certain level of entrepreneurial acumen. Later, a doctoral dissertation focused on how entrepreneurship is taught in college jazz programs. Professional experience and research have informed the creation of Arts Café, yet I do not see myself as an "entrepreneur" in the classic sense of the word. Steve Jobs or Elon Musk, people who identified a gap in the market or developed an innovative idea and created a business around it are entrepreneurs of a different nature. I also never attended business school. In teaching a course in which students run a business and look to me as the expert, I have always felt like an outsider.

What I have learned is that creating a student-run venture does not require a formal entrepreneurial background. It only requires the spark of an idea through the recognition of an opportunity and then realizing that idea. As I look back on the years I have taught Arts Café, there were certainly successes and failures. For instance, in a final reflection paper, a somewhat disenchanted student referred to Arts Café as an "unsuccessful business" with respect to profit. This characterization left me rattled. To be fair, it is valid from a financial standpoint, but I had never thought of Arts Café as "unsuccessful." Perhaps I am naive, but on the contrary, the fact that students enroll semester after semester and literally run a business in which they accomplish some astounding things qualifies Arts Café, from my perspective, as a success, irrespective of profit margin.

Arts Café is not purely a business. It is a business that college students run and a course in which they enroll. Therefore, the definition of success must be broadened beyond merely earning a profit. Personal fulfillment, creating a new idea, achieving goals, working as a team, and more can also be used to define success.

In short, the students and I are in this adventure together. While there are some decisions that can be universally acknowledged as wrong, like waiting until the day of a show to market it, everything else is fair game. It is an experiment, and there is room for testing new ideas. In that sense, I do not have to be the expert. I learn along with students, providing feedback and recommendations, but ultimately, I have to allow students to make their own decisions. This model is at the core of the student-run venture concept. The instructor may not be an expert in the subject area but may have an idea worthy of exploration, and the students explore it in a hands-on format with supervision. In a sense, an instructor recognizing an opportunity and capitalizing on it in the form of a student-run venture is in itself entrepreneurship.

Ideas for Teachers

Start small with one performance. Gather interested students in an initial meeting. Lay out your vision. Create job titles (talent scout, operations manager, etc.) and advise students on what their responsibilities will be. Continue to meet once a week, and as much as possible, let the students do everything, including brainstorming the name of the venue, making a list of the things needed for the performance (sound system, tables/chairs, a sign), considering who the artist(s) will be, etc. Give yourself a couple of months to plan. If the performance is a success, consider doing it regularly, once a quarter, for instance, and work up to a more formalized operation, like a student club or eventually a student-run venture.

Index

Printed and bound by CPI Group (UK) Ltd, Croydon, CR0 4YY

16/04/2025

14658434-0004